The Down & Dirty Guide To Adult Attention Deficit Disorder

By Michael Gordon, Ph.D. & F. Daniel McClure, Ph.D.

Published by   GSI Publications, Inc.
                PO Box 746
                DeWitt, NY 13214

Cover and graphic design by Jon Reynolds.
"Zippy" logo by Janet Junco.

The reader is advised that this book should not be considered as a substitute for the advice of a qualified health professional.

ISBN 0-9627701-9-1

GSI Publications, Inc.
P.O. Box 746, DeWitt, New York 13214-0746
Phone: (315) 446-4849 Fax: (315) 446-2012
Call us for quantity discounts on large orders.

GSI
PUBLICATIONS, INC.

Dedicated to our wives,

Wendy E. Gordon

and

Marion McClure,

for reasons that are obvious to us and probably even clearer to them. They both overflow with goodness and mercy.

Contents

Contents

Acknowledgments

Writing this book has highlighted for us once again how remarkably blessed we are by the expertise, encouragement, and kindness of our colleagues and families. Much of what we've written reflects their intellectual insights, editorial comments, clinical acumen, wise judgments, and saintly patience. This band of talented and supportive souls includes: Drs. Russell A. Barkley, Charles Cunningham, Sam Goldstein, Wendy E. Gordon, Wade F. Horn, Barbara B. Mettelman, Kevin Murphy, Kathleen Nadeau, Harvey Parker, Arthur Robin, Jerry Saffer, and Steven Tatar as well as Patricia H. Latham, J.D. We've also benefitted immensely from the editorial input and technical expertise of Mr. Bobby McGiver, Ms. Mary Daum, Ms. Susan James, Ms. Shirley Jean Lewis, Ms. Marion McClure, Mr. Jon Reynolds, and Ms. Gloria Ritter.

Two colleagues deserve special commendation: Dr. Mark A. Stein, from the University of Chicago, has been ever willing to focus fuzzy thinking and to administer injections of empirical reality. And Dr. Martin Irwin, Head of the Division of Child and Adolescent Psychiatry at the SUNY Health Science Center, helped enormously by being his challenging, knowledgeable, and friendly self.

Introduction

If you purchased this book, chances are you consider yourself to be inattentive and distractible. Assuming that you are indeed unusually inattentive (and not just unduly self-critical), a thick book filled with tables, charts, and wordy paragraphs won't help you much. So we've worked to make this book sufficiently interesting and brief that you'll finish it and find the information relevant to your daily life.

Rather than write detailed chapters about the identification and treatment of Attention Deficit Disorder (ADD), we'll present you with a series of "Principles." Each one deals with an important concept that will point you in the right direction as you find your way from identification to treatment. If your learning style is anything like ours, bold headlines and statements are easier to remember than dense explanations.

While we wanted to make the material attention-grabbing, we've worried throughout about becoming too simplistic, hokey, demeaning, or downright silly. Suffering from ADD is tough enough without experts treating you as if you were Forrest Gump. But we decided early to err on the side of the blunt and compelling. Consequently, be prepared for a rash of exaggeration, sweeping generalizations, and overly concrete directives.

You should take this information for what it is: broad statements regarding what we know about ADD in adults. Some of our guidelines may apply to your situation and others won't. We trust that you'll sift through our comments and extract what makes sense for you.

We admit from the outset that we're both intensely of mixed minds about this disorder. On one hand, we have no doubt that ADD is a legitimate problem that starts early in an individual's life and stays with him or her over time. We both have long track records of research, advocacy, and clinical practice in this arena. In country music terms, we were into ADD before ADD was cool.

But we're both deeply concerned that ADD is at risk of becoming yet another psycho-fad. Big trouble's in store if everyone who doesn't achieve as much as he'd hoped decides he's a victim of a handicap. You'll read some candid comments about what we see as the overselling of the disorder. We're also not hesitant about attacking the idea that having ADD is somehow glamorous.

What we're after here is a step beyond the domain of the typical self-help book. We've avoided simply describing the disorder uncritically and offering a rash of suggestions that are of only questionable validity. Instead, we wanted to make you acutely aware of the many pitfalls and cure-alls that swarm around the whole concept of ADD.

One last comment: While we've tried to be politically correct in our language, sometimes you have to just about torture a sentence to make it gender neutral. After wrestling with *he/she* and *he or she,* we decided to resort to the traditional *he* when all other conventions failed. In that about 80 percent of ADD individuals are male, perhaps we're justified.

Principle 1

Don't believe everything you hear about ADD from us experts today because tomorrow we could just as easily say the opposite.

To say that research has just begun in the area of Adult ADD is an understatement of monumental proportions. You could fit practically all the scientific articles about Adult ADD in your shirt pocket. While there are literally thousands of studies about attention deficits in children, only a relative handful are available regarding such problems in adults.

Although articles written prior to the 1980s probed the existence and treatment of ADD symptoms in adults, it has only been within the past 10 years or so that investigators began studying the disorder in earnest. When it comes to understanding a problem as complicated as Adult ADD, 10 years of exploration represents but a flicker in time.

Unfortunately, many are offering up bold statements about the disorder that are based far more upon speculation and guesswork than upon a solid foundation of scientific evidence. If anyone talks about Adult ADD with an air of absolute certainty and authority, we advise you to be wary.

It's not that we researchers know nothing about Adult ADD. Certain aspects are relatively clear to us. But most of what any of us have to say at this point flows not from proven facts, but from clinical experience and intuition. Some of our best guesswork emerges from extending research findings regarding ADD in children.

We begin our book with this caution to put the current state of knowledge about the disorder in some perspective. ADD in adults is a barely explored wilderness. Although we "experts" have some solid notions about what's involved in proper identification and treatment, we're all miles from being able to offer you certainties.

We also want to help you become a good consumer of medical and mental health services. Trouble brews when labels and treatments spring up before they've been thoroughly tested. Consider the advice you've gotten over the years regarding the health benefits of ingesting fish oil and oat bran and of avoiding caffeine and alar. All the fanfare around these prescriptions have dimmed in the face of more careful study.

Why did it take so long to figure out there is such a thing as Adult ADD?

For many years most assumed that ADD disappeared by adolescence. Professionals told parents of what were then called "hyperactive" children to be encouraged about the future: Just survive until your youngster reaches puberty and all will be well.

But then researchers systematically began to follow the lives of ADD children. They identified children in the elementary school years and tracked their progress into adolescence and young adulthood.

The results paint a much bleaker picture than most of us researchers and clinicians had anticipated. While the overactive behavior often diminished by puberty, many of the other symptoms persisted to a greater or lesser degree in at least two-thirds of cases.

According to these life-span investigations, children identified as ADD were a highly vulnerable group. Compared to non-ADD individuals, they were more likely to experience academic underachievement, poor job performance, drug and alcohol use, depression, and relationship problems. While not all ADD children still had ADD symptoms as adults, it was more common than not for them to experience ongoing adversity.

So the answer to the question, "What took so long?" is that clinicians initially judged persistence of the disorder primarily by keying on activity level. Most ADD children become somewhat less fidgety and physically active by adolescence. When research started looking at the overall adjustment of ADD children who have grown up, we realized that other features of the disorder usually endured.

Principle 2

Before you assume you have ADD, make sure you're not simply on the sloppy, spacey, hot-headed, or impatient side of life.

Show us someone who isn't occasionally inattentive and impulsive and we'll show you a corpse. All of us, even the most cautious of us, experience episodes when we're not as focused as we might be. We've all made hasty decisions or said things without thinking. Few of us make it through a week without being forgetful or distracted. All of us could do better if we only concentrated more and daydreamed less.

Some have personalities that predispose them to be especially disorganized or careless. Others have the ability to concentrate and plan, but are far more interested in pursuing creative whims or private thoughts.

Put plainly, it's normal to be inattentive and scattered. It's especially common when we're overwhelmed with responsibilities or managing complex tasks or dealing with powerful emotions.

Here's a list of "typical" characteristics associated with ADD. It's the sort of inventory that you'll see displayed prominently in magazine articles, on TV shows, or in professional materials:

"Typical" Characteristics Associated with Adult ADD

► Confusion	► Procrastination
► Forgetfulness	► Frequent job changes
► Impatience	► Poor concentration
► Distractibility	► Interpersonal difficulties
► Impulsiveness	► Job underperformance
► Sloppiness	► Poor control over temper
► Inattentiveness	► Low frustration tolerance
► Lack of discipline	► General underachievement
► Poor organization	► Trouble finishing tasks
► Low self-esteem	► Trouble maintaining relationships

We dare anyone to look at this list and not find a characteristic (or two or three) that hits close to home, at least some of the time.

The symptoms associated with ADD are all normal behaviors taken to extremes. Unlike symptoms of many other mental health problems, those exhibited by people with ADD aren't in and of themselves odd. Hallucinating the face of Elvis on your bathroom mirror or thinking that the CIA has rewired your brain—now that's weird. But ADD symptoms aren't necessarily unusual.

To make the point, we both made lists of things we've botched over the past month. Now, you might see this compendium as evidence that we're both candidates for medication. But, by any standard, we've done well for ourselves. Sure, we could do better if we were more organized and careful, but we've been blessed with more than our share of professional and personal success. So judge for yourselves:

Gordon's Most Recent Screwups

► Forgot to pick up clothes at the cleaner's. This had serious implications because of an early morning airplane flight to present a workshop. Had to run to the mall to buy new pants and shirts. Good thing the clothing store and tailor were open late that night.

► Drove to friend's house to deliver a recipe. Arrived safely but had forgotten recipe at home. Embarrassing and time-consuming.

► Promised youngest son to bring home science section of newspaper for a report he was writing. Damned article never quite made it into my briefcase.

▶ Colleague compared state of car interior to condition of certain streets in Bombay. Also embarrassing, but did motivate me to remove most of the offensive litter.

▶ Spent two hours trying to find a wrench I needed to fix the dishwasher. Sustained minor injury searching through workbench (didn't put razor blades away safely). Eventually found wrench, unaccountably, in drawer containing compact discs.

▶ Forgot to return mother's call. You don't even want to know.

McClure's Most Recent Screwups

▶ Promised to meet wife and daughters for lunch, but went to the wrong restaurant. I could have sworn she said we'd get together at . . .

▶ Gave two patients the same appointment time because I didn't write down the first one. Every clinician's nightmare.

▶ In talking with parents of a patient about local school issues, I blurted out that one of the politicians was a #@?&* Nazi. Fortunately, parents agreed wholeheartedly.

▶ Stored a tidy sum of money for Christmas presents in the glove compartment of my aging truck. Forgot about the mice that keep warm on the engine block at night. Mice used cash for nesting materials.

How do you know that ADD is for real and not just a cheap excuse for laziness and disorganization?

Fair question. The capacity to attend is like all other human attributes, from height to foot speed. For any given ability, most of us are within an average range, some of us are unusually good at it, and others fall greatly below average. This is called a normal distribution of abilities. When an individual falls way below average, we typically consider such an individual abnormal in that area.

Some abilities are nice to have but aren't crucial. You can generally get along just fine if you can't draw. You don't hear about a "Drawing Deficit Disorder" (at least we hope you don't).

You can also adjust if you're on the very low end of the scale for jumping or swimming or writing or any number of skills. Sure, you might not become a professional basketball player or a prize-winning author, but you'll still manage. In fact, you can have a rewarding life even if you're extremely limited in one or more ways.

When it comes to more necessary abilities, most of us have ways we can compensate. Nowadays you can be a horrible speller but still produce a reasonably clean document by using a computer spell checker. You might have a terribly poor sense of direction but live in an area where services are close by or buses are abundant. Perhaps you are devoid of mathematical capacity, but you've found a job that requires little computation.

To manage the demands of daily life, though, certain abilities are critical. Without them, even if you're capable intellectually and physically, you'll still seriously underachieve.

One of those vital qualities concerns the capacity to stop your behavior long enough to make good judgments and to finish tasks successfully. In order to accomplish nearly anything, you've got to keep yourself from responding to the irrelevant. And if you do respond to the irrelevant, you've got to bring yourself back to the job at hand. In other words, you must pay attention.

Self-control and attentiveness are not trivial attributes. They form a glue that keeps people stuck to tasks long enough to finish them. It helps us learn, organize ourselves, plan, analyze problems, and finish something we've started. If you can't produce, no matter how bright or competent you are otherwise, success will be hard to realize.

But the glue composed of attention and self-control holds more together than just what's involved in establishing ourselves as productive students or workers. It allows all of us to anticipate consequences, to maintain an activity level that's appropriate to the situation, to read social cues, to drive carefully, and to keep our emotions in check when those emotions are best restrained. If the brakes on your behavior are not working normally, you've got trouble across the board.

To claim that there's no such thing as impaired attention or self-control, then, would be in the same league as claiming that there's no such thing as severe limitations in the ability to see or to hear. Vision and hearing are both critical human abilities that, in a small percentage of the population, can be in abnormally short supply.

A characteristic of deficits in attention and self-control, of course, is that they're almost never immediately obvious. You can spot a person with visual impairments relatively easily. It takes only a few seconds of conversation to identify that somebody's hard of hearing. But ADD is a largely invisible affliction that is often no less disruptive than a physical handicap.

So the question in our minds is not "Is ADD a legitimate disorder?" There's ample evidence that attention and impulse control are human characteristics that, for one reason or another, can be severely limited in certain individuals. Researchers have also provided data that people with such low levels of attention and self-control have a different neurobiology than those for whom these characteristics fall within a normal range.

What we do worry about is people calling abnormal those abilities that actually fall within a normal range. We caution everyone to observe the distinction between ADD as a disorder and ADD as a personality style. Many of us are on the impulsive, inattentive, and disorganized side of life. All of us who reside on that end of the continuum could do better if we were more attentive and had fewer ADD-like traits. But that doesn't mean we necessarily suffer from a disorder. We might just have a bad case of being human.

So how far off the charts do you have to be before you reach abnormal?

That's the proverbial $64,000 question. If the ability to attend is a characteristic that is distributed across our population like height or weight, how do you decide how bad off someone's got to be before he's reached abnormality?

The problem, of course, is that this decision isn't all that clear-cut. There's no mark on a scale that we can point to and say, "This is precisely how inattentive you need to be for us to consider you abnormal." An attention deficit isn't like a cancerous mole that is bad news because it exists. Instead, it's an extreme along a continuum.

When you read about our suggestions for a proper ADD evaluation, you'll get a sense of how clinicians document abnormality. You'll find that we look for evidence that you've had problems throughout your life and that those problems, both in the past and present, severely hamper your adjustment.

Principle 3

Before you assume you have ADD, make sure you're not primarily depressed, anxious, physically ill, or odd.

Even if you are extremely inattentive, it doesn't necessarily mean you have ADD. The wildly inattentive are actually a hodgepodge of individuals. Why? Because the ability to concentrate is a notoriously fragile phenomenon. When humans become stressed in just about any way you can think of, one of the first things to be affected is the capacity to pay attention.

By "stressed" we're talking about any insult upon the body or mind. When humanoids are worried or upset or in physical pain or sad or overwhelmed or brain injured or hallucinating or intoxicated or traumatized by their past or angry or grieving or apprehensive, their attentiveness usually suffers. Most of us judge our level of stress at least in part by how disorganized, distracted, and forgetful we happen to be at the moment.

The delicacy of human attention explains why symptoms associated with poor concentration pop up all over our criteria for adult mental health disorders. If you look through our diagnostic manuals, you'll see those symptoms everywhere.

So the news here is that inattention is a feature not only of normal behavior but also of most forms of abnormal behavior. Here's a partial list of problems that have symptoms that can be mistaken for Adult ADD:

- ▶ Schizophrenia
- ▶ Posttraumatic Stress Disorder
- ▶ Anxiety
- ▶ Depression
- ▶ Manic Depression
- ▶ Panic Disorder
- ▶ Obsessive-Compulsive Disorder
- ▶ Various medical problems

Are you telling me that the identification of Adult ADD is just a crapshoot, or can you give me something more than cautions?

Don't worry. We'll offer some concrete suggestions for how to understand the difference between ADD and everything that can look like ADD. We just wanted to help you guard against jumping to the conclusion that you have ADD solely because you can be inattentive. As you'll read, you'll find all kinds of compelling reasons for seeking a formal evaluation. Read on.

Principle 4

You don't come down with ADD like you do a cold.

Adult ADD is unlike most other mental health problems in that the symptoms show up very early in life and stay with the individual with relative consistency. Some days will be better than others and some situations will usually be more successful than others, but ADD is always lurking.

Because ADD is a lifelong condition, one of the best ways to eliminate other possible conditions is to review your past. If you didn't show ADD-like symptoms as a child, the chances are you don't have ADD as an adult. You might have other legitimate problems, but ADD probably isn't one of them.

Does this mean I've got to understand ADD in children to understand ADD in adults?

Yup. But you're lucky. The concepts are straight-forward and, we think, sensible. They revolve around what we call *Indicators for the Identification of ADD.* If you understand these indicators, you can make reasonable judgments about how severe your ADD symptoms were as a youngster. You can also use them to assess your current situation.

Even with the help of these indicators, making sense of your early life is no easy task. With the passing of time comes the fading and twisting of memories. Matters aren't helped by the many changes in labels for the disorder over the years. A child considered a "dunce" in one era might be labeled "MBD" (Minimal Brain Dysfunction) in the next, or "Hyperactive" in another. But you've got to start somewhere, so let's discuss these indicators.

Indicators for the Identification of Childhood ADD

> ► **Impulsiveness**
>
> ► **Early Onset**
>
> ► **Consistency**
>
> ► **Extensiveness**
>
> ► **Severity**
>
> ► **Intentionality**

We're going to consider each of these indicators separately although, as you'll soon see, the concepts overlap mightily.

▶ Indicator #1: Impulsiveness

If you're going to travel back over your lifetime in a search for indicators of ADD, you need to know what to look for and where to look. For most of us, it's not hard to find examples of inattention or underachievement. As we've mentioned, most of us experience bouts of inconsistent performance at home and at school even if we're stone cold normal.

But what if we went through periods of fighting or skipping classes or engaging in delinquent activities or withdrawing from others? Could those have been early signs of ADD?

If I was popular as a child, would that have meant I didn't have ADD? Was my intense moodiness perhaps related to ADD?

How about the failing grades in algebra? Do they count as underachievement?

What if I wasn't especially hyperactive? Would that mean that I didn't have ADD?

All these questions ultimately boil down to a single one: Which class of behaviors are relatively unique to ADD and which are more common to other disorders?

The best answer we have to that question is as follows: What makes ADD children different from other children is their lifelong, intense, and debilitating impulsiveness. As a group, ADD children exhibit little self-control. They never seem to stop themselves long enough to consider the consequences of their actions, even when they really try.

The result of this intense impulsiveness is a life-pattern of underachievement and poor adjustment. ADD children are terribly disorganized and find it excruciatingly difficult to manage situations that require planning and careful preparation. To formulate a strategy and to anticipate obstacles, you first have to stop and think. Unless circumstances are unique, ADD patients don't often stop when stopping would serve them well.

Whether to noises around him or to cascading (but not strange) thoughts in his head, the ADD child responds quickly and without much consideration. The internal brakes that normally stop a person from responding to extraneous events often fail to perform their function.

As we mentioned earlier, overactivity and physical impulsiveness are more common in younger than in older ADD children. Young ADD children often don't sit still long enough to get anything accomplished. They often dash about, climb on everything, and show little regard for personal safety.

Parents of young ADD children are usually filled with stories of their children failing to anticipate consequences. Some accounts are dramatic, others more subtle and amusing, still others tragic.

They tell us about numerous visits to emergency rooms, avoidance of family gatherings and public places, untold damage to property and possessions, close relationships with security guards at shopping malls, distant relationships with neighbors, and hostile relationships with school-bus drivers.

We hear stories about helicopter searches in national parks for lost children, minor civil disturbances, toothpaste that never stays long in the tube, friends who get tired out by the ADD child's energy, and parents who swear that this child has stolen their best years.

We hear things like, "We barely survived his infancy," "We've never had a baby-sitter come back a second time," "My dining room table has holes from an electric drill my son wanted to experiment with," and the ever-popular, "He's really a sweet kid, but you don't want to know what I've thought of doing to him."

What are some examples of impulsiveness in a younger child?

We're hesitant to give too many vivid examples for fear that you'll think that all ADD behavior has to measure up to them in severity. *Not all ADD children are forever out of control.* But to give you a flavor for how impulsive some children can be, here's a fraction of a long diary of destruction one mother kept of her son's activities. These all occurred within the first six years of his life:

✓ Put blinds cord around neck & got twisted up. Neck red when rescued.

✓ Ripped dustcover off the bottom of TWO box springs, and the stuffing out from around the sides.

✓ Pushed mattress off the bed several times daily until we had to rope it to the box spring.

✓ Chewed on edge of two dressers. (Both were 22 years old and barely had a mark; now they look like something from the Salvation Army!)

✓ Pulled out all the drawers of dresser until it toppled over on top of him, trapping his legs.

✓ Sat on floor banging toys against drawers, leaving deep dents.

✓ Climbed up toy shelves inside closet, once breaking off shelf supports.

✓ Pulled curtain-draw mechanism from wall while "mountain climbing."

✓ Pushed whole-house humidifier into sister's door, making a large hole.

✓ Pulled heating register plate from floor repeatedly. Bob drilled & screwed it down, but Kevin could STILL pull it out, screws & all.

✓ Climbed up shelves of particleboard bookcase (75 lbs.) to climb onto adjacent dresser, causing bookcase to fall over. It smashed Fisher-Price Zoo, but luckily, sister had moved from that spot a minute before.

✓ Pulled down toys & room decorations that were hanging from ceiling.

✓ Ran wind-up race car over dog's tail, then let go, entangling dog's hair in wheels. Much of poor canine's hair had to be cut off.

✓ Age 4 before learned how to put on coat. Age 5 before he could manage zipper. At 6, cannot/will not tie sneakers.

✓ Walked out of preschool classroom several times, until even other 3- & 4-year-olds in class kept

---

an eye on him and told the teacher when he started to leave.

- ✓ SPUN hamster exercise ball with hamster inside— teacher furious, but controlled. "In all my years of teaching, I've never had another kid like HIM!"

- ✓ Kicked out of pre-beginner swimming lessons after FIRST lesson; no-refund policy waived. "Please, Mrs. M., don't bring him back."

- ✓ Jumped into deep end of swimming pool before Bob ready to join him. Kevin was found doing "Dead Man's Float," but rescued quickly.

- ✓ Hid under display racks of clothing stores. Wouldn't respond to name.

- ✓ Set off fire extinguisher in back hall of grandparents' house. Took two hours to clean up the mess.

- ✓ Got into liquid dishwasher detergent. Smeared on face, some got in eyes—red and VERY irritated. Would not cooperate to rinse it out under sink. Went to E.R.

- ✓ Broke window in rental house three days after moving in, by throwing toy at sister. (He missed.)

- ✓ Stuck finger in large floor fan. Ran screaming into bedroom, hiding behind bed. Large gash, but very, VERY, lucky. Another trip to E.R.

- ✓ Picked up spray can of insecticide, finger on push-button, directed at face. Grabbed away just in time.

- ✓ Got into ALL perfumes and colognes, spraying over self and bedroom furniture. Almost a week before house didn't STINK. Age 6.

✓ If task is novel or interesting, he can stay with it for hours. But routine tasks (brushing teeth, picking up toys, getting dressed, etc.) cannot be accomplished. I even had to feed him dinner at age 4—he just could not concentrate.

✓ <u>Generally he has a happy, sunny disposition. But anything can send him into a tantrum, and the trigger is not the same every time.</u>

While this little boy would seem to anchor the far end of the continuum, many of our patients have histories of a similar sort.

What's an example of impulsiveness in an older child?

A teenager went on a Boy Scout overnight camping trip deep in the woods of the Adirondack Mountains. The first morning, he was sitting by the fire and decided to make himself hot chocolate. As he was pouring the boiling water into his cup he heard a noise and looked away. During the distraction he continued pouring the water and didn't pay attention to the fact that it was missing the cup and landing in his shoe. He suffered serious burns on his foot and had to be carried over several miles of wilderness for medical attention.

What's the worst possible situation for an ADD child?

If you wanted to design ADD Hell, the worst possible place to stick an ADD child, you'd come up with a typical American classroom. After all, what does our system do with children who can't concentrate on anything other than tasks that are extremely compelling? We require them to spend hours every day concentrating on tasks that are often anything but extremely compelling. School is a monumental struggle because of all those requirements to sit still, fend off distractions, and complete work.

And what school activity is the worst of the worst for the ADD child? What's his Kryptonite, Achilles' Heel, and Waterloo all wrapped into one? Without any question whatsoever: Homework.

If homework were outlawed, we're sure the recorded rates of ADD would plummet. Think about the amount of planning and organization even a simple homework assignment involves:

▶ Writing the assignment down accurately
▶ Remembering to take the assignment sheet home
▶ Remembering to take the necessary books and papers home
▶ Concentrating long enough to complete the assignment accurately even though you struggled all day at school and you now hear basketballs bouncing outside and the voices of friends chattering

- ► Remembering to put the homework in your book bag
- ► Remembering to take your book bag to school
- ► Getting the assignment out of the book bag and into the hands of the teacher

While this process is easy enough for most children, ADD youngsters are prone to be tripped up at any and all points along the way.

If impulsiveness is the hallmark of ADD, why is it called Attention Deficit Disorder?

It's a long and confusing story. But here's the short version: This same set of symptoms has had a remarkable number of names attached to it through the years. Even now Attention Deficit Disorder (ADD), Attention Deficit Hyperactivity Disorder (ADHD), and the old-fashioned "hyperactivity" are all in common use, even though they refer to the same problem.

Although the term "hyperactivity" was a popular label for several decades, it lost favor in the 1970s for several reasons. First, research began to indicate that what differentiated hyperactive from nonhyperactive children wasn't necessarily the sheer quantity of behavior. What really set hyperactive children apart was the poor quality and control of their behavior. Investigators started homing in on the hyperactive child's inattention, poor concentration and planning, and difficulties complying with rules. Eventually, the powers that were changed the label to reflect the focus on these qualitative aspects of the child's behavior, particularly deficits in attention.

So for several years we used the label "Attention Deficit Disorder (ADD)," which could come in the two flavors of "with Hyperactivity" and "without Hyperactivity." Although many of us were perfectly happy with this designation, those same powers decreed that there should be just the one term, "Attention Deficit Hyperactivity Disorder." ADD can now come in the the "Predominantly Inattentive Type," "Predominantly Hyperactive/Impulsive Type," and the ever-popular "Combined Type."

For our books on children, we've stuck to this ADHD label because it's the most official. Also, hyperactivity is a common feature of the problem in young children.

But for this book on adults, we decided to bend to the popular winds and use ADD. After all, it's used in the titles of nearly all the books and articles on the subject, and hyperactivity isn't as typical in adults. We felt that the field is baffling enough without introducing a new term to the popular literature.

The main point here, though, is that these terms are used interchangeably. Don't be thrown if someone uses ADHD instead of ADD. It's the same disorder.

By the way, it's unclear how long even the ADHD label will stay official. Most of us in the research community would have been happy if the term had been changed altogether and replaced with one that focused more on impulsiveness.

Where does this impulsiveness come from?

You've probably been bombarded by a slew of theories about the causes of ADD symptoms. We sure have. We've heard about vitamin deficiencies, various chemical imbalances, poor parenting, too much yeast, and too little education.

The bottom line is that most people have ADD more because of genetics than because of any other single factor. Other forces can cause ADD (especially pregnancy- and birth-related complications), but they are all far less likely causes than heredity. So the chances are that if you're unusually impulsive and inattentive, you've had a blood-relative or two with similar tendencies.

Exactly what it is that gets passed on genetically is an open question. The most popular theory as of this morning is that individuals with ADD have under-functioning frontal lobes. This explanation makes sense because the frontal lobes, located in the top front section of the brain, are thought to be intimately involved in what are called "executive" functions, such as inhibition, planning, and organization.

Our crack about the theory "as of this morning" simply reflects the ever-changing nature of science and speculation. We've seen literally dozens of explanations come and go over the past 20 years. The frontal lobe hypothesis is a good one, but we wouldn't be at all surprised if it's revised or supplanted by another.

You should also keep in mind that, at this point, theories about the causes of ADD aren't terribly relevant to treatment. You don't offer a therapy that's different for someone with family-based ADD than for someone whose symptoms likely stem from low birth weight or from oxygen deprivation at birth.

While you understandably will wonder why you've got the symptoms, you'll need to accept: (1) that you'll likely never know for sure, and (2) even if you knew for sure, it probably wouldn't change the treatment.

You should also know that ADD's high hereditability is why many of us clinicians who were trained as child psychologists or child psychiatrists are now seeing adults as well. We couldn't avoid it. In feedback sessions to parents regarding their ADD child's evaluation, we'd frequently be asked the following question: "This all sounds sensible and hopeful for my son, but what about me? I was exactly the same when I was younger, and I'm still having the same problems. Can you help me?" Apples really don't fall far from trees.

Now if impulsiveness is the key to ADD, are all ADD children boundless, thrill-seeking blurs of motion?

No. Some youngsters are of the more fidgety than zooming variety. They might not get out of their seats, but they're forever fiddling with pencils, getting distracted by noises around the room, blurting out answers, or doing three things at once (but taking none to completion).

An articulate college student, Brad, described his impulsiveness this way: "All through my life it's been like my head is filled with five TV's that are all turned on at once. I 'watch' one for a little while and then get distracted by another." It wasn't that Brad was waylaid by the intrusion of crazy thoughts from these "televisions." They weren't telling him to return to Jupiter or smoke the chandelier. He simply couldn't turn off responding to the competing thoughts and ideas that were popping into his head.

We want to emphasize the point again: To be considered ADD, you must have been impulsive and/or overactive as a child. While you don't have to have been running nonstop, evidence must exist that your brakes weren't working normally, even if the impact showed up in more nonphysical ways.

What if I was highly inattentive but not at all impulsive or hyperactive?

Individuals whose problems have far more to do with inattention than with impulsiveness form a distinctly different breed. In fact, current information suggests that those who are primarily inattentive shouldn't even be considered in the same category as those who are impulsive and hyperactive.

Children who are primarily inattentive (sometimes called ADD without Hyperactivity) are often described as being spacey, underaroused, and sluggish in processing information. They don't often have the social or conduct problems that impulsive children experience, nor are they as likely to have a family history of the traditional ADD with Hyperactivity.

While scientific information is scant about primarily inattentive individuals, clinicians will often follow a different diagnostic route in dealing with them. When someone is referred to us with complaints that focus on poor concentration in the absence of impulsive/hyperactive behavior, we're especially intent on finding answers to the following questions:

▶ Is the inattention possibly tied to significant emotional problems?

As we indicated earlier, when people are exceedingly anxious, sad, stressed, preoccupied, obsessive, compulsive, hallucinating, or panicky, they have trouble concentrating. Any clinician worth his salt will look especially carefully at these factors when people come in with complaints that focus primarily on inattention. Of course, he will also explore emotional issues even if the individual is highly impulsive since such problems are rampant in ADD adults.

▶ Are problems concentrating tied to learning problems or intellectual limitations?

It's hard to pay attention if whatever you have to learn makes no sense to you. Pretend for a moment that you had to spend the day trying to read Russian (and you had no Russian-language skills). Do you think you'd be attentive for long? No way. You'd be looking out the window in nothing flat. That's how academic life can be for children who have specific learning problems. They must force themselves to focus on words they have trouble reading, or on sentences they can't understand well, or on math problems whose solutions elude them.

If explanations for poor concentration don't flow from the answers to these two questions, a diagnosis of ADD without Hyperactivity (designated in the official lists as "ADHD Predominantly Inattentive Type") might be warranted. Such youngsters, despite at least normal intelligence, are slow in breaking down and processing information.

For those of you with computer experience, here's an analogy: It's like the Predominantly Inattentive (ADD without Hyperactivity) child has an old 286 processor and is trying to run Windows software. The program eventually loads, but it can take forever.

What we're telling you here is that a diagnosis of ADD without Hyperactivity follows from a process of elimination. If better explanations can't be found in the realms of social/emotional problems or learning disabilities and the problems are serious, such a diagnosis can be justified.

Can girls be impulsive enough to warrant a diagnosis of ADD?

Girls are rarely referred to ADD clinics. In ours, approximately 15 percent of referrals are female, although that number is rising every year. Boys are so much more likely to be referred that some question whether girls can have ADD symptoms, or at least to the same degree as boys.

Before we start citing research findings and statistics supporting the notion that girls can have ADD, read what a mother wrote about her now nine-year-old daughter. (While we changed the name to protect the innocently impulsive and corrected some of the grammar, the account is unvarnished.):

"We have always been aware that Cindy can be determined to do things without thinking about safety. Until Cindy was 4, we basically set it up that someone was always with her on a one-to-one basis. We still have someone watching her constantly. Although we see a great improvement in this area, I do not feel as comfortable with Cindy understanding limits as I felt her siblings did at the same age.

"At 8 months, Cindy tried to climb out of the crib. We changed cribs. We put latches on doors, hooks on doors, plugs in outlets, etc. Nothing seemed to contain her.

"At age 1 year, she burned herself severely by plowing through three barricades to get at the wood stove handle in the time I walked 20 feet to give a sibling a school note. A week later, she reached up toward the electric stove and even though we yelled, "No, Hot," and she yelled, "No, Hot," she touched it anyway and got burned again. To this day we only use the back burners on the stove.

"At age 1 1/2, Cindy received stitches when she tried to catch up to her siblings who were just starting to climb a hill. She didn't look where she was going and tripped.

"At age 3, Cindy swung from a bannister to unlatch a kitchen door hook that led to the garage. More injuries.

"During her pediatric checkups, I talked to the doctor about Cindy's behavior. He said some children's curiosity overrides their sense of danger.

Principle 4

"At 3 1/2, while we were both raking leaves, she put her rake down and went toward the side of the house. I followed. In a span of a minute she ate three berries from a burning bush. I called poison control and they said to give her syrup of ipecac, which I did.

"At age 6, she tried to save a mole that our cat had captured. The mole bit her and drew blood. I called both the pediatrician and our family physician who recommended to have the mole tested at the health department, which we did.

"Recently at a baby-sitter's, Cindy would not leave their pet alone. Cindy said it bit her. Even though we've discussed animals and being kind to them, at times Cindy does not seem able to control herself enough to leave them alone.

"The other concern we have for Cindy is school. During first grade, Cindy struggled academically. An advantage she had was being in a small class of 17. She seemed to be able to keep up, but the teacher said she was concerned about Cindy's chances in second grade. This school year, her behavior has improved, but she's less able to grasp the curriculum. Cindy's inattention is a consistent problem.

"Cindy is an energetic and happy child. She requires structure and positive reinforcement, which we give and have asked the school to provide."

In many ways Cindy was a typical ADD girl referral. Despite her history of accidents in the home, she wasn't so impulsive that the school was especially upset with her. The teacher did, however, note many examples of Cindy's distractibility and poor judgment. She also described her as vivacious, talkative, immature, and dreamy. But the teacher made no bones about how

---

Principle 4   37

much she adored this appealing little girl. She found her far too cute to be upsetting.

What prompted the referral for Cindy was her slow academic progress. Beyond her inattention, she also was somewhat limited intellectually. The teacher described her as slow in picking up concepts. This scenario is perfectly in line with the conclusions of our research and those studies conducted at several other institutions: Slow academic progress in the context of moderate behavior problems will spur parents and school to seek ADD evaluations for girls. For boys the impetus more likely comes from concerns about intensely impulsive and oppositional behavior.

Our ADD girls generally fall into two groups: One contains youngsters who are of at least average intelligence and can hold their own with any ADD boy as far as the capacity for trouble is concerned. The most disinhibited child we've dealt with was a six-year-old girl. She also met criteria for conduct disorder because she took a bat to several cars parked along her road.

The second and larger group contains children like Cindy. They have long histories of moderate impulsiveness coupled with academic slowness. Adults are slower to refer them because they're not as much trouble to manage and they take a longer time to fail and, therefore, to attract attention.

We're sorry, but there's little other hard evidence we can offer about ADD in females. Theories, conjecture, and diatribes are flying about, but almost no data so far. We know that girls can have ADD and that the nature of the disorder is essentially similar across genders.

What's likely is that the thresholds at which identification occurs can differ. Girls can have ADD even though they show somewhat fewer problems than ADD boys.

▶ Indicator #2: Early Onset

ADD is unlike nearly all other child mental health difficulties in that the problems surface early in life. Except for developmental disabilities, almost all other child mental health problems appear after the age of seven. The early blossoming of ADD partially explains why so many researchers feel that it has an especially strong neurobiological underpinning.

The "early onset" criterion doesn't mean that all ADD children must show symptoms in the hospital nursery. While some mothers describe their babies as hellions from conception forth, most ADD children are characterized as having been good babies. It's only when their walking about leads to parental decrees of "Don't touch" or "No" that problems inhibiting begin to surface. What starts as the expected "terrible twos" never seems to end.

While there are wholly supportable reasons why symptoms might surface later in childhood, most ADD children show problems early and often.

If I didn't show any ADD symptoms as a young child, does that mean I don't have ADD?

In most cases, the answer is yes. But, predictably, exceptions to the rule are common.

Here are some credible explanations for why ADD can appear later:

▶ **Sheer brain power** can help you make it through the first several grades without severe underachievement. If you're unusually smart, you can memorize easily and figure out ways to compensate. But high intelligence only lasts until demands mount for completing longer-term tasks. This usually occurs around fourth grade, but in some school systems or for some more mildly impaired individuals, they don't hit the "wall" until later.

▶ **Remarkably competent/together parents** can skillfully work around the child's impulsiveness and minimize opportunities that symptoms will interfere with achievement.

▶ **Remarkably overwhelmed parents** are often too caught up in other matters to notice the symptoms. Parents who don't set limits and establish expectations for self-control will have few opportunities to observe their child coping with rules.

▶ **Child has no preschool experiences** or has preschool experiences in either unstructured or highly structured and enriched settings.

▶ **Coexisting problems** (like speech and language delays, hearing impairments, physical illness, or adjustment reactions to traumatic events) grab more attention or are seen early on as possible explanations for the ADD symptoms.

These explanations for a later appearance of problems may be justified, but be careful. Unique intelligence or environment aside, most *bona fide* ADD children will show some evidence of the disorder at least by the end of the preschool years.

▶ Indicator #3: Consistency

ADD differs from most other disorders in its consistency over time. While day-to-day or minute-to-minute behavior can vary widely, the ADD child's average behavior stays relatively stable from month to month and from year to year.

We clinicians get a sense of ADD's consistency when we talk to parents about the impact of family trauma on their children. After detailing the disruptions of deaths, divorces, family moves, and financial woes, parents of an ADD child will add: "These problems bothered our son and made matters worse. But, regardless of our family situation, Johnny's always been Johnny."

It's the "But Johnny's always been Johnny" quality that marks a chronic, lifelong, and hard-wired condition. Sure, external events may have made matters better or worse, but the troublesome traits have always been present and in force.

Parents of children who have other kinds of problems tell stories with more abrupt startings and stoppings of symptoms. An anxious child may float along fine until he encounters worrisome situations or individuals. Children reacting to trauma usually show long stretches of normal behavior that are interrupted only by the impact of disruptive events. And children whose symptoms are best understood as reactions to inappropriate schooling will have educational histories that show sharp eruptions of failure amid a general picture of adjustment and achievement.

▶ Indicator #4: Extensiveness

Just as we clinicians expect ADD to generally characterize a child's behavior over years, we also require that the symptoms make themselves known across most of the daily routine. The notion is straightforward: We want to identify only children who have problems that span their everyday lives. If a child's behavior is truly abnormal, his difficulties should surface in most circumstances.

How could we agree that you had ADD as a youngster if you attended to all of your classes except for math? Would it be reasonable to consider your childhood as marked by ADD if you misbehaved at home but complied in school? What if you only had trouble dealing with peers or siblings?

From our point of view, you have to marshal convincing evidence that problems with impulsiveness and inattention were more than just a summer fling or passing phase. The problems associated with ADD are so much at the core of how someone operates that they interfere much of the time.

Children whose difficulties are limited to very specific circumstances usually have non-ADD sorts of problems. Often they're related to reactions to certain events or to impairments associated with other disorders.

Like most rules in life, however, this one is easier to deal with in the abstract than in the concrete. Only severely impaired youngsters are impulsive always and everywhere. The average ADD child will comply in many daily situations.

Actually, it's to the eternal frustration of parents and teachers that ADD youngsters are consistently and intensely inconsistent across situations and time. This variability also sets the youngster up to be judged as lazy or unmotivated. "Why could he do it yesterday but not today?" The teacher assumes, understandably, that he just doesn't care.

In fact, there's a certain pattern to when an ADD child will comply. It's usually easy to spot. If you want to predict whether or not an ADD child will behave, look at the amount of incentive and what we'll call the *rule/supervision ratio.*

Incentive exists if . . .

1. The task at hand is more compelling than almost anything else around at that moment.

and/or

2. There is some predictable and meaningful reward for compliance with clearly stated rules and/or some predictable and meaningful punishment for non-compliance with clearly stated rules.

As for incentive, if it's really worth the ADD child's while to delay, he'll more likely find a way to hold impulses in check. How much incentive is necessary depends on what we've dubbed the *rule/supervision ratio.* For ADD children (not to mention just about everyone else in the world), situations with lots of rules require lots of supervision. Conversely, free play opportunities, where there are few rules, require less supervision. Supervision essentially involves the efficient dispensing of incentives.

So when will an ADD child comply? Either when there are few rules or when there are many rules but ample supervision.

If you were an ADD child who could run around a farm situated far from a main road, you would probably play without incident. You'd likely also get along fine if you were with a wholly indulgent grandmother loath to set rules. Ditto if you had ADD but you were placed in a special classroom in which the teacher was always nearby to make the expectations clear, keep you motivated, and make it worth your while to comply.

But now they've placed your ADD self in a class of 30 other children with a teacher who can't spend his day ministering only to your needs. Trouble will surely follow. The same goes in the mall when Mom needs to look after two other children and pay for purchases.

The incentive factor and the rules/supervision ratio allow us to make sense of obedience in children who are generally disobedient. The inconsistencies of an ADD child's behavior tend to be related to these two factors.

▶ Indicator #5: Severity—Isn't anyone normal anymore?

Time magazine recently sported a cover proclaiming, "Disorganized? Distracted? Discombobulated? Doctors say you may have Attention Deficit Disorder." The phones in our clinic rang incessantly for days with requests for evaluations and medication.

Public awareness is no doubt helpful in educating everyone about the existence and legitimacy of the disorder. Parents who might not have understood why their bright and motivated child was failing miserably can now explore ADD as a possibility and get appropriate help. Teachers who had heard about the disorder but had little relevant information might now know where to look for assistance. Administrators and politicians might become more attuned to the sheer numbers of individuals who might need resources. And you—you might have gotten answers to questions you didn't even know you should be asking.

Many of us, especially those of us involved with national ADD advocacy groups, have been deeply immersed in that effort to gain public attention. Judging from the remarkable number of recent TV segments and magazine articles, we've done the job well.

Has the movement succeeded too well? Perhaps. We're both afraid that ADD, especially the adult variant, will go through a period of overexposure during which everyone and their blood relatives will figure they're not achieving up to potential because of this disorder. While no doubt some will actually have the problem, even more will latch on to it as yet another excuse for perceived under-attainment of success.

Because research can't offer clear markers for the disorder, the potential for abuse is boundless. Ultimately, individuals who truly have ADD will lose because the disorder, if we're not careful, will become pegged as another in a long string of mental health fads, alongside "codependency" and "repressed memory."

If we sound a bit agitated, it's not just because Rush Limbaugh has lined ADD in his sights. We've noticed in our recent workshops a militancy about ADD among some attendees that we haven't seen before, even among politically active parents. Therapists have become upset with us when we've wondered aloud whether it makes sense, for example, to diagnose a successful lawyer as having ADD just because he struggled in school or has to work particularly hard to keep his office organized.

The reaction we've been getting amounts to the notion that there's a little ADD in all of us and a lot of ADD in some of us. The argument continues that mental health professionals should assume that a patient with ADD complaints, even if he drives to our offices in a Mercedes and has advanced degrees, might still function more effectively if he were more attentive and organized. It's our responsibility, at least as we're told, to identify that problem and treat it as a disorder.

Unless we reserve the ADD label for the truly impaired, we fear that we will end up trivializing the disorder and treating personality traits as mental illness. We feel we have a responsibility to be conservative in setting thresholds for diagnosis and in making absolutely certain that there is evidence of significant impairment. Even though arbitrariness looms large when establishing that point of "significant impairment," a competent evaluation allows at least a good stab at making that determination.

Because it derives from decisions about severity along a continuum, lines have to be drawn in the sand. No unimpeachable standards exist for deciding what "serious" or "severe" means. Line drawing is a mixed blessing. It allows for clear criteria, but it also establishes the risk of not including those who hover about demarcations of normality. It also means that some children on the fringes of average will get pegged as abnormal.

Here are some indicators clinicians use to judge impairment in children:

- ▶ **Ratings** by credible adults that the child's behavior falls well into abnormal ranges (somewhere around or below the fifth percentile for child's age and sex).
- ▶ **Chronic underachievement** relative to native abilities. Not necessarily multiple grade failures, but grades far below what one would expect given a child's intellectual ability and desire to achieve.
- ▶ **Symptoms are pervasive** across most settings and are consistent over time.
- ▶ **Chronic impairment** of peer relationships that leads to isolation.
- ▶ **Deterioration in self-esteem** because of academic failure and social difficulties.
- ▶ **All the standard, common-sensical interventions** at home and school haven't worked.
- ▶ **Risk of physical injury** is high for both the child and others.
- ▶ **Impulsiveness** has lead to stealing, truancy, and legal actions.

While not all the criteria we've listed above must be present, most should stand out. In essence, to consider your childhood as characterized by ADD, you must have compelling evidence that you had problems with attention and self-control that appeared early in your life and have been long-standing, pervasive, and relatively consistent over time. These symptoms must have been serious enough to cause you problems that were far more debilitating than one would expect given your intelligence and motivation to achieve. They also had to be largely resistant to the reasonable efforts of your parents and teachers to help you improve.

Does this mean that I had to be failing, in jail, or sleeping on a heating grate to consider my youth as marked by ADD characteristics?

All problems vary in their severity. ADD is no different. Some who have ADD suffer extreme impairment while others are less affected. But even in its mildest form, ADD causes serious underachievement relative to one's abilities. You couldn't have been all that impaired if, for instance, you have an average IQ and performed at or above grade level without any special services or unusual efforts on the part of your parents and teachers.

Now you could convince us that you had serious problems if you had an average IQ and performed at grade level, but only because of Herculean efforts by you, parents, teachers, siblings, and the National Guard. You could even convince us you had ADD if you were at grade level but had an IQ in the Superior Range and should have been at least a year or two ahead of schedule. Yet those are special circumstances in which "normal" isn't all that normal. In our approach, psychiatric diagnoses are assigned to individuals who show the abnormal and not just the "slightly off."

How about in adulthood? Can you own a Lexus and still have ADD?

Now we're in the territory that spawns the most heated of arguments within the community of ADD researchers, practitioners, and advocates. As you've gathered from our discussion so far, we're decidedly conservative in our setting of thresholds. We feel strongly that, to warrant a diagnosis, someone has to show consistent and serious problems adjusting. ADD isn't a label that should be affixed to everyone who must work harder to achieve or who fails to realize each and every dream. Few of us would escape inclusion in the ADD circle if the criteria were so loose as to incorporate successful people who wished they could be more successful. And if everyone who's made an ass of himself upon occasion qualified for a diagnosis, forget it.

How bad off can you be if, despite your inattention and disorganization, you're managing a lucrative business? If you're a highly accomplished real estate broker, should you seek consideration for a diagnosis of ADD because you haven't been able to complete an MBA program that you enrolled in because you wanted to and not because you had to? Is a label what you need if you find yourself working 10 hours to accomplish what most others manage in 8? Is ADD and a pill the answer if it's becoming evident that you've just about maxed out on your talents as an administrator or lawyer or politician or researcher?

"Hold it!" you scream. "Maybe I'm successful, but it comes at a monumental cost to me and to my family. Sure, I have the trappings of affluence and accomplishment, but I'm never home, I'm always depressed and miserable, and my relationships with others are strained at best. And, in case you're wondering, I've tried everything I can think of to compensate and it just isn't working." Well, now you're describing a degree of impairment that might qualify as sufficient to take the ADD plunge. If you've achieved, but it's nearly killed you in the process, maybe the diagnosis is justified.

A gentleman recently came for an evaluation who might fit into the category of "gifted and prosperous but ADD nonetheless." We use the words "might fit" advisedly because we're frankly not completely convinced. Decide for yourself:

Stan is an extremely accomplished businessman who could buy out the two of us with the cash in his ostrich-skin wallet. Despite a lifelong history of disorganization, distractibility, and impulsiveness, he parlayed his prodigious mathematical abilities and a $500 loan from his father into a sizable investment firm. He also became involved in politics and served several terms on the school board.

On the darker side, Stan just ended his third marriage, has little contact with his two children (one of whom has ADD-like school problems), and has been in psychotherapy of one form or another for 15 of his 45 years. He's also worked his way through many a bottle's worth of psychiatric medications.

Stan has never been able to understand why he has to struggle so hard to keep organized and on task. The analyst's accounts of inner conflicts or the marriage counselor's attributions to fears of commitment never rang true. More conceivable to Stan was his father's characterization of him as "the luckiest lazy fool on the planet."

Thanks to his good fortune in business, Stan has hired a small army of secretaries and assistants whose duties largely entail the monitoring of his every move. He still has lost literally hundreds of thousands of dollars because of his failure to record transactions and generate appropriate invoices. These losses, while financially painful, are even more debilitating to his self-esteem. It seems that no amount of swimming pools, sport cars, or trips to the Riviera can overcome his frustration or convince him that he's anything other than an incompetent.

Even though we might entertain the possibility that ADD is a legitimate diagnosis for a Stan, we want to reiterate our general position: Except in rare cases, a person should be diagnosed as having ADD only if he or she has a history of these symptoms and can provide evidence of ongoing and debilitating impairment. Short of that, we advise caution. You might well gain more by accepting yourself for who you are than by looking to psychiatric labels to account for unmet goals.

I have serious ADD-type problems, but I've found ways to adjust. Are you saying I don't have ADD because I can compensate?

When we debate our colleagues on these issues, they routinely invoke the memory of Nelson A. Rockefeller. As you might remember, he was the grandson of the legendary oil tycoon, John D. Rockefeller. After serving four terms as governor of New York State, Nelson Rockefeller became vice president under President Gerald Ford. He attained such prominence even though he had a problem, called dyslexia, that made it almost impossible for him to read. Because he was smart and extremely rich, he was able to work around his disability and, to say the least, do OK for himself. (He died under some curious circumstances, but that's another story.)

Nelson Rockefeller is brought up to buttress the following line of argument: Here's a fellow who couldn't read yet, thanks to unlimited resources and constant compensation, he adjusted well. Are you saying that he wasn't dyslexic because he could achieve?

No. Rockefeller was a treated dyslexic who required extraordinary and ongoing assistance to function at that level. Like anyone else with a disorder that responds to formal treatment (and not just everyday life adjustments), he still warranted the label. Were it not for his energy, talent, and problem-solving attitude, he probably would have been just your run-of-the-mill multimillionaire.

Our substantial nearsightedness serves as another example: Although both of us wear corrective lenses, we still have a definable vision problem. Without that intervention we'd be in rough shape.

By this point we're sure you're catching our drift: Beyond requiring a childhood history of ADD, diagnostic decisions turn tightly on questions of "How bad are the symptoms?" and "How much do you have to go through to compensate?" If ADD symptoms are in evidence but not terribly debilitating and not all that hard to work around, you might want to consider yourself just on the sloppy, disorganized, or hot-headed side of life.

► Indicator #6: Intentionality

One of the most important ADD indicators is also among the hardest to pin down. It has to do with judgments of what we call "intentionality." When we diagnose a youngster as having ADD, we're in effect saying that a substantial portion of his poor compliance occurs for reasons that go beyond willful disobedience.

Typically, when parents arrive for the evaluation, they have already traveled through a maze of other theories for their child's problems. Understandably, they first assume evil intent on the child's part. "He's just irresponsible and looking to give me a hard time," they'll say. When the problems persist despite lectures and all manner of extravagant rewards and dire punishments, parents consider other causes: marital stresses, single parenthood, sibling rivalry, mother-in-law intrusions, poor teaching, too few vitamins, too many vitamins, and food allergies. Sound familiar?

So when parents call for an appointment, they've about exhausted their supply of non-ADD explanations. They've come to realize that their child fares poorly even when he tries. They begin to suspect causes other than those related to rebelliousness.

The term "ADD" essentially describes a youngster whose misbehavior is severe but often largely unintentional. When he gets into trouble, he genuinely seems swept away by his impulses, and there's a sincerity to his clueless shrug in response to the question, "Why in the world did you do that?"

The non-ADD child who seriously misbehaves often seems in control and fully aware of the consequences. While he has the capacity to control himself, his anger and defiance leads him to oppose at every turn.

We're not saying that even severely ADD children don't frequently misbehave with some intent. Children by nature are often disobedient and oppositional. It's just that the ADD child's misbehavior more typically stems from poor consideration of consequences. People come to judge it as flowing more from malice without thought than from malice aforethought.

I went through your criteria for ADD in childhood and I hit almost every one. Does that mean I have Adult ADD for sure?

No. A childhood history of ADD is necessary for a diagnosis, but it's not all that's needed. To qualify for the diagnosis, you have to experience currently that "significant impairment" we described earlier. In other words, the ADD symptoms must now be seriously interfering with your ability to cope.

One way to find out if you're in the right diagnostic church is to take a look at the road map we've printed on the next page. It will give you a sense of the questions a clinician has in mind when he meets with you to discuss the possibility that you have ADD.

The Road to a Diagnosis of Adult ADD

Did you have a history of impulsive/hyperactive and inattentive behavior that:
1. Showed up early in life (before age 6 or 7 unless you were very bright or in special circumstances)
2. Appeared consistently over the years and across most routine situations
3. Led you to underachieve significantly relative to your abilities
4. Couldn't be accounted for by trauma, severe family dysfunction, or serious emotional problems

If "no," unless you've got a good explanation for why you didn't meet the criteria (such as unique academic environment, family situation, and so on), pursue other avenues or consider possibility you're normal.

If "yes," do problems with impulsive and inattentive behavior still interfere significantly with your ability to function in the workplace and at home?

If "no," consider possibility that you've successfully compensated for impulsive and inattentive style.

If "yes," are you sure that your problems aren't more easily understood as resulting primarily from:
1. Serious anxiety and depression
2. Formal psychiatric disorders (such as obsessive-compulsive disorder, manic-depressive illness, or schizophrenia)
3. Medical problems
4. Learning disabilities

If "no," make sure clinician carefully reviews all your symptoms and considers other explanations.

If "yes," (and professional agrees), chances are you've got ADD. You then need to move on to identify any other problems that might be joining ADD.

Adult ADD in the flesh

Because we've beaten the requirements for a diagnosis of ADD nearly to death, let's change course and describe some real people we both agree meet criteria for Adult ADD. In reading descriptions of these people you might get a flavor for the symptoms and the level of impairment we think is required for the diagnosis. *But please keep in mind that they are simply case examples. The folks we describe below don't represent standards or benchmarks for ADD.*

Case History—Gerald

"I quit high school two months before graduation and got married. I never liked school, hardly ever completed any homework, and always just slid by. I got drafted into the Army and surprised myself by passing the GED (General Education Development) test on the first try without studying. I knew I was smart, but I never could do well in school.

"After about six months of being stationed overseas, I applied for a Hardship Discharge because I missed my wife. I didn't get it. When I came home on a seven-day leave, I ended up staying for three months and got in serious trouble. After that I decided I liked the Army and, when my stint was up, I re-enlisted for six more years.

"I did fine as a tank commander. The thing I liked about the Army was that the rules were clear and, if you did a good job, you got rewarded. Most decisions were made for you.

"Because my wife got sick with arthritis real bad, I got a discharge to take care of her. Leaving the Army was the worst thing I ever did.

"After the Army, I had a hard time keeping a job. I worked a number of part-time jobs for a few years, but I never could stick with something long enough to make anything out of it. For a while I had a position with a federal agency, but it was just too boring. I found myself wanting to 'fast forward' through every workday.

"It got so I would drive to work just dreading the day, so I quit. Then I worked in a delicatessen, which was OK, but I couldn't get along with the owner, and again I quit. I worked for awhile processing insurance claims, but there was too much paperwork, and I had to work in a little cubicle. It drove me nuts.

"Now I have what I think is the perfect job. I do maintenance for a company that owns various properties. I set my own pace, I go to different sites all day, and there's always something new for me to get into. There's not much future in this job, and it certainly isn't challenging but, for me, it's manageable. The problem is that there's not much money to be made and the bills are piling up. And even in this job my boss complains about my forgetfulness."

Case History—John

"I always struggled in school. I grew up in the rural South, where they didn't have a lot of patience with disruptive children. I mostly remember that, whenever the teacher would get after me, she'd call my mom. When my father got home, he would discipline me severely.

"I was kind of a smart aleck. My mouth got me into a whole lot of trouble. It seems I spent much of my childhood standing in corners either at home or at school. The other kids used to love to get me revved up and excited. I was always caught in the middle of the mischief.

"Even though I was talented at football and basketball, my poor grades always kept me off varsity teams. I got a job in a gas station in my junior year of high school. I liked making money more than I liked school, so I quit.

"Soon after, I was drafted into the Army and went to Vietnam. I was a good combat soldier, but when I returned from Asia I didn't adjust well to the military routine. It was just like school, in trouble all the time. Nothing serious, just breaking the rules. I did manage to get my GED before I was discharged.

"I wanted to go to college on the GI Bill, but I was married and needed to work. It didn't seem like I could ever find a job that suited me. Although I was a hard worker, I always felt like I just didn't fit in. I had no idea what I wanted to do, but I knew it wasn't what I was doing. My problems holding a job put strain on my marriage. In fact, it really caused our break up.

Principle 4

"After the divorce, I started taking courses at a community college. For the first time I actually did well in school. The course work was more interesting, and you could work at your own pace. I did best in subjects I was interested in, but I managed to do OK in the others also.

"After two years I was able to transfer to a major four-year university. I majored in psychology, which was really interesting, and graduated near the top of my class. I have decent work now in a state hospital, but I have trouble with my paperwork and administrative forms. One of the reasons I've come for an evaluation is that I'm afraid I'll lose my job if I don't get more organized. What bothers me the most is that I've done everything I can imagine to improve my handling of all the papers and reports.

"I'm married again now. My present wife is much more understanding of my difficulties. There's kind of a running joke in the house about my absent-mindedness. They won't let me cook because I tend to get sidetracked. I've started a couple of fires on the stove. It's real hard for me to finish the projects I start around the house, which has caused some stress. But it's the problems at work that worry me the most."

Case History—Molly

"It's torture for me to talk about school because it was so painful. Not only was I heavy and freckled, but I was also spacey as could be. I never felt like a part of things. When a girl doesn't make good grades in elementary school, people think there's something wrong with you.

"All through school I tried to do the 'right' things and be popular, but it never worked. I'm embarrassed at the way I behaved a lot of the time. I never thought about things before I went ahead and did them. My thoughtlessness led me to do things that were just plain stupid. I'm lucky I didn't end up a teen mother.

"High school was better. Once I gave up on trying to be popular and just accepted my situation, I made better grades. But I was always lonely and out of the mainstream. By senior year I really threw myself into schoolwork and did well enough to get accepted into a nursing program in college.

"I did well enough in college. I had some good friends who were helpful and it was a small school. Actually I was sad when I had to graduate because I liked the routine and I knew exactly what was expected of me.

"After I finished, I never could really find my niche in the nursing profession. I worked as a public health nurse, but that didn't work out. For awhile I was a nurse in a nursing home. They let me go because I was too disorganized. I went to work for an insurance company reviewing claims, but that was a disaster.

"I got married shortly after leaving that job. I am incredibly fortunate because my husband can support us on his income. Having two children provided me with some 'cover' because I could avoid formal employment by staying home with the kids. Not that it was easy keeping track of all the the various schedules for after-school activities. But children don't usually fire their mother for being scattered.

"With the children older now and more self-sufficient, I've run out of excuses not to be working. Besides, with things the way they are, I have to get a job to help pay for college bills. I really want to work, but I'm terrified of going through another phase of job misery. I felt real competent as a stay-home mother, and I'm not sure my self-concept can take more failures on the job. But I did start a new position last week at another nursing home. Wouldn't you know that my new supervisor is already making comments about me being too disorganized?"

Case History—Sharlene

"I'm an elementary school resource teacher for learning disabled students. I've been working there for three years. I've just received my third consecutive negative performance evaluation by my supervisor. I'm now on probation.

"As you can imagine, there's a ton of documentation you have to complete when you're a resource teacher. Mine is always late and incomplete. My tardiness has delayed some of the children getting services they require.

"Worse by far is my mouth. Things come out of it that are just stupid. Not crazy or mean, just inappropriate for where I am. Another teacher just told me that I need to engage my brain before I open my mouth. I've been reprimanded several times because of language I've used in the classroom.

"Although people seem to like me fine at first, I can turn them off in short order. I'm not a good listener and I blurt out embarrassing things that cross my mind. Tact isn't my strong point. It seems I spend half my life apologizing and feeling guilty.

"Aside from my job problems, I'm in debt. I'm an impulse shopper, and I'm now working with a credit manager to keep from going bankrupt. I've also been in several automobile accidents. They were all caused by my inattentiveness.

"If you're wondering if I've thought maybe I'm just a hostile person or have emotional problems, you should know that I've been in every therapy you could think of, including psychoanalysis with a guy who actually had a couch and smoked a pipe. I've gotten in touch with feelings galore, but I'm still forever screwing up big time."

What if everyone thinks I'm ADD but I think I'm just fine the way I am, thank you very much?

You might be right. As you can tell, we believe the ADD diagnosis makes sense for only a very few people, not for everyone in a zip code.

But you also need to consider the possibility that your friends and family aren't all that off base. It's hard to acknowledge you've got a problem, especially if you're the proud and independent sort. That's admirable.

Nonetheless, it may be that, despite your efforts and those of people who care about you, you really are sinking. You might be failing in college even though you know you're smart enough and working hard (but inefficiently). You might be faring poorly at work, perhaps in large part because of disorganization and poor concentration. Your home life might also be unsatisfying due to tensions caused by your inattention and impulsiveness.

It's human nature and perfectly legitimate to first look outside of yourself to explain personal failures. Maybe the teachers *are* boring and incompetent. Maybe your husband *is* overly concerned about neatness. Maybe the boss *is* a poor manager who hands out confusing assignments or has unreasonable expectations.

But, then again, those people telling you to look into ADD might be right. Perhaps you really do have a problem that's been hard for you to overcome.

You only really know if you have ADD by asking the question and sincerely looking for the answer. If day after day, year after year, you constantly and seriously underperform because of inattention and poor self-control, it might be time to check it out.

If I'm bumping into these indicators of yours, what do I do now?

If you're convinced you meet the essential ingredients for a diagnosis of ADD, your next step is to consider the possibility that you also are affected by additional problems. And then it's time to get yourself evaluated professionally. We'll cover both issues in the next two sections.

Principle 5

ADD is a disorder that loves company.

In case we haven't confused you enough, here's another wrinkle: Even in children, ADD is typically joined by other problems. Between 70 and 80 percent of ADD youngsters referred for evaluations have some other identifiable disorder. The most common are behavior problems (usually intense defiance or delinquency) and a variety of learning problems. Also teaming up with ADD can be anxiety disorders, depression, and a host of other symptoms.

By adulthood, the picture doesn't change much. It is important to understand that having ADD doesn't mean you can't also be depressed, anxious, or whatever. Actually, if you have ADD, you're even more likely to have other disorders. When we evaluate adults for ADD we search high and low for these other coexisting problems. But usually we don't have to look far.

Even if, as a child, you were only ADD pure and simple, new problems might well have emerged over the years. Our point here? By the time an individual with ADD reaches adulthood, add-on problems are more likely than not. You can't go through life saddled with a highly impulsive style without paying an emotional price.

Too often clinicians, after identifying one problem, stop looking for others, even though having more than one disorder is common. The errors travel in both directions. A practitioner might correctly identify the presence of depression in an adult, for example, but not consider that the sadness is due, in part, to ADD-generated poor self-esteem. And a "specialist" in ADD might do a fine job in discovering the ADD, but completely miss the presence of substance abuse or anxiety or obsessive-compulsive disorder. The identification of mental health problems is not an "either/or" proposition. While we'd like to pretend that human problems assemble in neat little packages, it just isn't so.

What are the problems that most often join ADD?

First, a brief lecture on psychiatric disorders. Mental health problems can be roughly divided into two groups: Internalizing and Externalizing. Internalizing disorders are those problems that cause inner pain. The difficulties the individual experiences are expressed through physical symptoms or through upsetting feelings of anxiety and depression or through disruptive rituals, intrusive thoughts, or impaired judgment and logic

Externalizing problems, as the name suggests, may be upsetting to the individual, but they also affect others. Antisocial behavior, ADD, and substance abuse are the most common of these disorders.

Now, as we've indicated, individuals with ADD are vulnerable to experiencing not only ADD-related problems, but also those associated with other disorders from both the Internalizing and Externalizing realms. If you don't tend to anticipate consequences well, it's far more likely you'll get into trouble with authorities for breaking rules. Certainly not all ADD adults have problems with the law (it's probably closer to about 25 percent), but the risk for antisocial behavior is higher.

One of our ADD teenage patients was just arrested for shoplifting. Did he plan his crimes? Not at all. He saw a CD in the corner of the store and impulsively stuck it in his coat. With typical ADD inattention, he didn't look around to see if he was being observed or notice the guard near the door. He saw, he liked, he took.

Individuals with ADD often make terribly incompetent criminals. They don't plan well or anticipate how their crime might be discovered. Their inattention to detail can make for easy detection.

ADD adults are also at significant risk for dependency or addiction. Some scholars have theorized that ADD adults are more apt to "medicate" themselves with drugs or alcohol. Others see the higher incidence of addiction related simply to the telltale impulsiveness so much at the core of the disorder.

Regardless, a clinician must know whether substance abuse is a problem for you. It's essential both for understanding your situation and for formulating a sensible treatment plan. Simply put, it's hard to treat someone who's stoned or drunk much of the day.

How can you be impulsive and anxious or depressed at the same time?

If you have ADD, life can seem like a series of random events chained together with no apparent logic. You forget important things. You miss crucial meetings. Because you're impulsive, you're frequently in trouble before you even realize what you've said or done wrong. Even when you do manage to get it right, you're not always certain how you pulled it off.

If you're not sure how to *make* good things happen, you certainly aren't confident in your ability to *prevent* bad things from happening. You always walk around wondering if you've screwed up again. That can make you anxious and depressed.

But you can also be depressed for reasons that go beyond the frustrations of being ADD. You might have desperate problems keeping your mood out of the mud hole because of past losses or traumatic events or any number of other reasons.

How do you know if you're seriously depressed and anxious? Some of the signs and symptoms are listed below:

▶ Constant feelings of sadness, emptiness, or worry
▶ Loss of pleasure in daily activities that should be pleasurable
▶ Too little or too much sleeping
▶ Almost daily sense of fatigue and loss of energy

- ▶ Trouble concentrating
- ▶ Ongoing sluggishness or agitation
- ▶ Frequent thoughts of death or suicide

If any of these symptoms, especially the last one, describe your situation, *let it be known immediately.* You can tell your partner, contact your doctor, call a hot line, visit the counselor at the employee assistance program, or mention it to a member of the clergy, *but notify someone without fail.*

Isn't ADD often joined by difficulties that, while not formal psychiatric problems, still cause all kinds of trouble?

You better believe it. There's a whole range of personality problems that can eventually take on a life of their own. While they might have gotten an early boost from the ADD, these ways of coping and relating to others can become embedded in somebody's character and prove hard to shake. Life also has a way of introducing other forces and events that give rise to unhealthy coping.

Let's say Fred has had a full dose of ADD and all its repercussions from day 1 of his 40 years. By his teens he had formed the opinion that he was incompetent and that those in authority were unkind and dismissive. He becomes soured on life and develops an angry and oppositional way of interacting with others. Over the years his ornery and belligerent approach to coping becomes an ingrained style that, incidentally, isn't relieved much by medication.

Or how about 33-year-old Diana (not the princess) who spent a lifetime trying to overcome her extreme inattention and disorganization? She wore three alarm watches on her left wrist, showed up to meetings often two hours early (so fearful was she of being late), and rarely dated or went out with friends, preferring instead to stay at work to prepare for the next day. Diana's physician even wondered aloud whether she had obsessive-compulsive disorder.

When her ADD was eventually identified and treated with medication, Diana found it profoundly easier to keep herself organized. But it took years for her to work her way out of her over-focus on keeping ordered and scheduled. That style had become a part of her makeup and required time and the heavy blasting of counseling to dislodge.

Just because these personality accommodations might not become disabling enough to trigger a psychiatric diagnosis doesn't make them inconsequential. As you'll read in the sections on treatment, they warrant close attention.

Principle 6

Don't assume anything unless you've had a credible evaluation.

While you now have a sense of what clinicians look for when they conduct ADD evaluations, you won't be able to formally evaluate yourself or someone else without professional assistance. Even if you have not a doubt in your mind that you suffer from Adult ADD, you still need an outside opinion from someone who can take an objective look and prescribe a sensible course of treatment.

C'mon. If I think I'm ADD, why can't I just get some treatment? Why do I have to mess with a bunch of shrinks?

ADD is a complicated disorder that can easily be misjudged. It's too easy even for professionals trained in this area to miss the problem or to overidentify it. As we've indicated throughout this book, there are no sure-fire indicators for ADD that are a cinch to spot.

The criteria for Adult ADD leave ample room for interpretation. How severe is severe? Was your childhood as disrupted as you think it was? Are you sure that some of your symptoms don't reflect other problems? On your own you can't fairly answer these kinds of questions any more than you could fly solo in the diagnosis of a heart ailment or other medical condition.

Are we just drumming up business here for our colleagues in the helping professions? Not at all. If there were a quick self-test for ADD that would eliminate the need for a professional evaluation, be assured we would have described it many pages ago. Such a magic test just doesn't exist.

Also, don't forget that you'd take risks launching into treatment without first making sure you really do suffer from the disorder. First, you could be wrong and not get the real help you need. You could be overlooking possible medical conditions that underlie your problems. You might get yourself into treatments for ADD that you really don't need. And, finally, you might be right about having ADD, but miss additional problems that also should be addressed.

It's not that we don't understand why people want to dash into treatment. Individuals with ADD are an understandably frustrated bunch. They are constantly confronting their limitations and want a cure NOW. But coping with ADD is like coping with any other of life's hardships: You can't find effective solutions until you first have a complete understanding of the problem.

How do you find a competent clinician?

The search for decent professional help may well be the most difficult of all the tasks you'll face. Because Adult ADD is a disorder in its infancy, there simply aren't that many professionals of any stripe who have been trained to handle these referrals. Even in large cities, you'd be lucky to find any more than a handful of clinicians who specialize in Adult ADD. And if you actually locate such a rare bird, you might be disheartened to learn that you can't get an appointment for six months or more.

Fortunately, more clinicians should be on the market soon. Whenever the demand for services is high, the supply inevitably increases. And, trust us, the demand for ADD-related services is overwhelming.

But, for now, you'll have to be persistent in your search for a suitable clinician. It will be frustrating. You'll run into clinicians who are too skeptical about the disorder and clinicians who have a reputation for seeing ADD in anything that moves. You might run into practitioners who are knowledgeable but creepy, and others who are approachable but limited in the scope of their knowledge. You'll also encounter perfectly sophisticated and reasonable clinicians with whom you just don't feel comfortable.

Here are some strategies for compiling a list of possible candidates for your business:

▶ Learn a little about ADD so you'll know some of the right questions to ask.

▶ Call your local Mental Health Association for ADD specialists in your area.

▶ Call a local parent support group chapter (such as CH.A.D.D. or ADDA, see page 203 in the Resource section). People in these organizations are often remarkably knowledgeable about local resources. They've been consumers themselves and have a well-honed sense of who's competent and approachable.

▶ Call a child psychologist or child psychiatrist. Often they end up dealing with Adult ADD because the parents of their child patients request service for themselves.

▶ If there's a nearby medical center, call it. Often medical centers have specialty clinics within their psychiatry or pediatrics departments that can either serve you or refer you to the best clinicians in the region.

What Brand of Clinician Should I Hire?

You will notice that we don't suggest that any particular brand of health care provider will necessarily be more helpful to you than others. In our experience, competency and decency are not guaranteed by initials after a name or by fancy titles. We've seen practitioners with master's degrees show great expertise in evaluations. We've also dealt with full professors of psychology and psychiatry who are sorely lacking in evaluation skills.

You should know, though, the various disciplines that are mostly likely engaged in ADD-related services for adults. Each brings a different background and therefore a different set of skills and philosophies to the evaluation:

▶ **Psychiatrists** have medical training and are in a good position to assess the medical end of things. They can also prescribe any medications that will be required in the treatment of ADD. They're especially helpful if you have a complicated medical background. What they are usually unable to offer is a testing-based diagnostic workup.

▶ **Psychologists** are schooled in both educational and psychiatric approaches to handling learning and emotional problems. While they do not prescribe medications, they do offer the spectrum of psychological services essential in many cases for a sound evaluation and diagnosis. They have specific training in behavior management techniques and psychotherapy. As a group, they are not trained to assess medical disorders.

▶ **Internists/Family Practitioners** are physicians who are not formally trained in psychiatry or behavioral health. Typically they deal only with the medical end of an individual's psychiatric problems, usually after another discipline has completed a full evaluation. Nonetheless, we are seeing more and more internists and family practitioners who are developing an expertise in ADD. An advantage to working with family practicioners is that they know you well and can coordinate your care.

- ▶ **Neurologists** specialize in evaluating and treating disorders that are associated with measurable brain abnormalities. These include problems such as epilepsy, tumors, and multiple sclerosis. Some also will deal with ADD, even though the brain abnormalities are less observable.

It may surprise you to find that no one group of health care providers has a lock on managing ADD. In our opinion, this is to your advantage. While we have indeed seen people whose symptoms are so extreme that essentially a well-trained orangutan could diagnose their ADD, most individuals require a thorough and broad evaluation.

So what am I looking for in a clinician?

We have put together a list of what we feel to be essential qualities of a competent clinician. Most of these are common-sense, but are worthwhile stating nonetheless.

The practitioner you choose **should:**

- ▶ Be knowledgeable about Adult ADD either through professional training or continuing education (workshops, seminars, training institutes, etc.).
- ▶ Take time to talk to you and to those who know you best.

- ▶ Explore all the possibilities and not just focus on whether or not you have ADD.

- ▶ Be able to demonstrate to you some of his training and expertise in the area by describing his overall approach to diagnosis and treatment.

- ▶ Have a reputation for working with other professionals, where appropriate. Often the role of the clinician is not only that of diagnostician or treatment specialist, but also that of *coordinator and manager.*

- ▶ Advocate for you, but also not hesitate to tell you if you're out of bounds.

The practitioner you choose **should not:**

- ▶ Hand you a prescription before he asks your name.

- ▶ Act like a "cheerleader" for ADD and see ADD as an appropriate diagnosis for anyone with a blood pressure.

- ▶ Treat ADD lightly or dismissively, and seem too quick to discount the possibility that you have ADD.

- ▶ Have a quick answer for everything. (There's much to be said for an honest "I don't know.")

- ▶ Lack interest in all facets of your life, that is, your physical status, work situation, family life, etc.

- ▶ Be unable to explain the rationale for his approach to diagnosis and treatment.

- ▶ Speak unintelligibly by using jargon and medical terms that are confusing.

How can I tell if someone meets these specifications?

Ask him. And ask others. Practitioners have reputations you can evaluate.

Don't be shy about asking questions. Unfortunately, most people in this world spend more time contemplating which car to buy than which doctor to consult. Because this is a very serious decision, be thorough. Life's too short and this is all too serious to trust your fate to a jerk.

Credentials and decency aside, choose someone you can afford. You really don't want surprises at the end of a billing cycle. Any credible practitioner will fully describe your financial obligations up front.

Some practitioners will have a fixed fee for a package of services. Others charge by the hour. Find out what those charges are and what the upper limit will be for the services discussed. It doesn't hurt to have these arrangements in writing. You also should check with your insurance company and get confirmation of their coverage.

What should I expect in a comprehensive evaluation?

Because there's no "standard" evaluation for Adult ADD, practitioners will vary in their approaches to assessment. While there's no universal protocol, certain elements should be present. From our perspective, all competent evaluations should, at a minimum, include the following elements:

- ▶ In-person interviews with the patient
- ▶ In-person or phone contact with significant others
- ▶ Completion of standardized rating scales by the patient
- ▶ Completion of standardized rating scales by significant others
- ▶ Administration of at least a brief (screening) IQ test

Depending on the nature of the case and the background of the clinician, the evaluation may well include one or all of the following:

- ▶ Psychological testing (personality tests, computer tests of attention, full IQ testing, learning disabilities tests, neuropsychological measures)
- ▶ Vocational assessment
- ▶ Physical examination

Notice that we put contact with significant others (parents, spouses, children, and friends) in the list of essential components. Often the best information comes from the people who have to live with the ADD adult. Frequently they have thought more carefully about the impact of the symptoms. It's also often easier to see problems in others than in ourselves.

By this point you know why it's so important for us to contact parents, past teachers, and anyone else who might have known our patient as a child. The bulk of the ADD diagnosis rests on documentation that the symptoms were present early in life. The more information we can gather about those first years, the more confident we can become about our conclusions.

What we didn't list as an essential element in all evaluations was the need for a physical examination. We didn't because it often occurs outside of the actual ADD evaluation. *But everyone who is assessed for ADD should have had a thorough physical examination within the past six months.*

The physical exam is critical for several reasons. First, certain medical conditions can produce ADD-like symptoms. You need to eliminate those explanations before proceeding to those that focus on psychiatric or neuropsychological factors.

Another reason for getting a physical is that individuals with ADD are notorious for adopting the sentiment that "If I just ignore it, it will go away." They tend to be inconsistent in keeping up with routine medical care and often develop habits that can be injurious to their health. Any excuse for getting you to that checkup is worthy.

Finally, if you are identified as having ADD, stimulant medication could well be recommended. No adult should be started on such a medication without a thorough physical examination. Some of the medications that might be prescribed can raise blood pressure, interfere with sleep patterns, or conceivably reduce the threshold for seizures. (For a more thorough discussion of side effects, see pages 121-123.)

For females, that examination should include pregnancy tests. While no evidence is available about the effects of low doses of stimulants on fetal development, no one would want you to take chances.

What can I do to make the evaluation more efficient and accurate?

Step 1: Educate yourself.

Learn as much as you can about ADD. Go to support group meetings, lectures, and bookstores. Learn enough to know the types of questions you should ask your clinician. We know we keep emphasizing the importance of advanced knowledge, but it's simply critical. (See our Resource section at the book's end.)

Step 2: Say what you mean.

Use your own language. Don't try to communicate with psychiatric jargon. It doesn't help us at all. Psychiatric terms have technical meanings to clinicians that you might not intend. For example, it is common for people to say that they are "anxious" about an event. In fact, they are "eager." The word *anxious* has a highly specific psychiatric meaning, which has little to do with eagerness.

Similarly, many use the word "depressed" to describe anything from mild disappointment to pity to abject despondency. If you were sad about something that happened, say you felt "sad." Whatever best communicates how you felt is just fine.

Step 3: Prepare a "life story."

Because so much hinges on information about how you were as a child, it's important to gather evidence any way you can about that time in your life. The more details and examples you can generate, the more valid your evaluation will be.

Because specifics are hard to come up with when you're sitting in a doctor's office, prepare ahead by reviewing your life a bit and by asking around. Here are some options:

► Talk with your parents and ask them what you were like as a child. Discuss your early schooling and how they saw you as a youngster. Write it down so you can bring the notes with you.

► Look for old report cards. We've found that almost all parents, even those well on in years, save a folder with your name on it. In it are report cards, drawings, and other memorabilia that might be informative. No, you don't have to bring the ashtray and potholders you made in art class.

► Get ahold of any past psychological test reports or other evaluations that might have been conducted along the way.

► See if any of your past teachers are still around. Even though you thought your teachers were so ancient as to be at the brink of death, most of them weren't actually that old. Some have survived and can provide testimony.

Step 4: Be honest.

It's not easy to sit down with some stranger and tell him that you drink too much or got arrested several years ago or hear voices inside your head or lose your temper often. Most of us don't relish the opportunity to detail our most serious faults and embarrassing vices. But you know the drill here: The more you hide, the less help you'll get. Clinicians may have many talents, but mind reading isn't one of them.

Remember that all practitioners are bound by ethics regarding confidentiality. What you say to them will be kept strictly private. If you have questions about how they maintain that confidentiality, ask them. If there are specific matters you don't even want your wife or husband or parents to know, tell the clinician.

Also take comfort from the knowledge that there's not much you can tell a seasoned practitioner that would shock him. Like members of the clergy, we've about heard it all. It will be harder for you to talk about upsetting events than it will be for us to hear about them.

Being honest also means not consciously withholding or shading information that might be seen as evidence against your having ADD. To say the least, there are worse things in the world than finding out that you don't have ADD.

Step 5: Don't overinterpret.

We've noticed that many people who've just learned about ADD begin to interpret everything that's ever happened to them as symptomatic of the disorder.

Fuzziness around criteria for identification of the problem makes this exercise an easy one.

Now it may be that awareness of ADD really does change how you see yourself and explain things that were previously mysterious. But it's best not to do the clinician's work for him by tying all your history and behavior to ADD. Just tell him the facts of your life and experience. Leave it to him to decide whether they're symptomatic. Don't start every sentence, "Now another sign of my ADD is that . . ."

Step 6: Line up "witnesses."

As we mentioned earlier, some of our best information comes not from our patients, but from those who live with them. You probably won't report all kinds of things that we should know about. You might not recognize them as unusual or troublesome. To you, they are simply the way things are.

Yet to others these events might be interpreted in a different light. Here's an example: A fellow indicated that he never seemed to have enough time to do the things he needed to do because he had too many responsi-bilities. "I just need more hours in the day to get everything done." His wife had a different view. "He has all kinds of time to finish his chores, but he just putters about aimlessly for hours at a time and gets nothing done. It's his lack of awareness of time passing that causes the problem."

Involving a spouse or partner has the added benefit of helping him or her develop a greater understanding of your behavior. A spouse who enters the consultation room complaining of anger toward a mate who is "selfish," "preoccupied," "undependable," and "lazy" may leave the room with a more sympathetic view. A more understanding partner can work wonders on an individual's ability to cope with ADD.

So speak to your spouse, parents, or others about being involved in the evaluation in some way. Since children can also provide important insights, don't forget them.

Some have advocated involving employers or supervisors in the diagnostic process. Obviously, this is a very different issue from involving parents or spouses. While job evaluations and performance reviews may be good to bring in, actually involving the employer may not be in your best interest. This is a decision you should make. In many instances, it may be better to include the employer after the diagnosis has been established, rather than before (see page 189).

Step 7: Be patient. (Right!)

Telling someone with ADD to be patient is somewhat like asking a leopard to shed his spots. Try to remember that a thorough evaluation takes time. We know you're eager to learn the results. For years you've known that *something* was wrong, but you never knew what it was. You always assumed it was "just the way you were" or that you were indeed lazy, irresponsible, and an overall bad apple. And now you may well have something that not only has a legitimate name, but also a highly effective treatment!

While the feedback holds potential for relief, take the evaluation a step at a time. Even if you are convinced that you have the disorder, give the clinician a chance to perform his tests, make his calls, and conduct his interviews. You're paying this guy a lot of money to do his job. Let him do it.

Are there psychological tests that I should expect the clinician to administer?

Although there isn't a specific "test" for Adult ADD, we routinely recommend that a battery of psychological measures be administered. Results from these tests not only help with the diagnosis, but also can provide valuable information for treatment planning and vocational guidance.

In addition to psychological tests, we occasionally refer our patients for a formal vocational assessment. This is particularly helpful for individuals with serious difficulties in the workplace or who chronically find themselves in exactly the wrong job.

Psychologists are the health care professionals who are trained to conduct testing. Here are the kinds of tests you might be asked to take:

▶ **Intelligence testing** is especially important in cases where we need to document how much below your abilities you're performing . Questions often loom about intellectual giftedness, limitations, or unevenness in performance. The standard test of intelligence is the Wechsler Adult Intelligence Scale—Revised. It consists of 11 subtests measuring a broad range of cognitive abilities. While it does provide an IQ score, its biggest value is in the identification of specific cognitive strengths and weaknesses. Most of us, unless we have a good reason, will administer brief screening measures and give the full IQ test only when it is warranted.

▶ **Achievement testing** assesses academic skills such as reading ability, spelling, and mathematics. Such a pegging of academic level is valuable in that it may weed out possible learning disabilities, or help guide you in your career search by identifying specific academic strengths and weaknesses.

▶ **Personality testing** is designed to evaluate an individual's coping style. It's especially helpful in determining whether or not someone has psychiatric problems. This is crucial in identifying certain mental illness whose symptoms may mimic ADD. This testing also helps identify certain personality traits that may be an asset or liability in the workplace.

▶ **Behavior rating scales** are popular methods of obtaining normed data for the diagnosis of ADD. These are scales that contain listings of various problem behaviors and symptoms. The rater is asked if such a problem is present and, if it is, how serious a problem it poses for the individual. These scales are relatively quick, user-friendly methods for obtaining information. An added benefit is that ratings can also be obtained from others regarding the behaviors exhibited by the individual.

► **Tests of attention** are available to assess specific abilities in the areas most central to ADD. The most widely used and researched of these is the Gordon Diagnostic System (GDS). The GDS is a computerized instrument that administers a number of tasks that require concentration, attentiveness, and delay for successful performance. It has been proven to be highly effective in evaluating ADD in children and adolescents. However, its applications to the diagnosis of ADD in adults is still under scrutiny. The same holds for other commercially available computerized measures such as the TOVA and Conners Test. A diagnosis of ADD should never be based solely upon results of a computerized test.

► **Vocational assessment** is an important but often overlooked component of a complete evaluation of ADD in adults. The symptoms and secondary effects of ADD can have potentially devastating effects upon career selection, job placement, and worksite performance. These tests, coupled with the other components of the evaluation, can be instrumental in helping you capitalize on intellectual strengths, academic aptitudes, and personality traits. Most psychologists are not well versed in vocational assessment and career planning. As a result, you may have to go to a separate agency for this testing.

Don't be shy about asking your provider whether or not psychological testing might make sense. In dealing with a disorder as complex as ADD, it's hard to have too much quality information. If your clinician cannot conduct certain of these procedures, he can certainly help you with referrals to individuals who can.

What kind of feedback should I be getting from the clinician?

The ultimate goal of an evaluation is to empower the patient with accurate information that leads to a sensible treatment plan. Unless you have that information, your chances of finding and sticking with help will narrow.

The only way to become fully informed is to get clear and meaningful feedback from the clinician. Nothing is so complicated in this process that a competent practitioner can't explain it to you in plain English. *Whatever you do, don't just sit there nodding your head if you don't have a clue what he's talking about.* Here are some related tips for making the most of the feedback session:

► Don't tolerate "psychobabble." If your clinician uses words or phrases that you don't understand, don't hesitate to ask for clarification. Simply say, "What did you mean when you used the word . . . ?" *Never* be embarrassed to ask for clarification.

► Bring a tape recorder so you can record the feedback session. Because the clinician will be spewing forth gobs of information, it's good to have the tape to refer back to when it dawns on you the next day that you really didn't understand everything he presented. Also, you can play it for other family members, your teachers, or anyone else who might benefit from the information.

▶ Before you leave the interview, say to the clinician, "OK. Let's just review what you're telling me so I'm absolutely clear about the plan." Don't leave until you are confident you understand completely his conclusions and suggestions.

▶ If the clinician suggests some further evaluation, ask when it will occur, how long it will take to complete, and specifically what information it will provide.

Should I receive a written report?

Absolutely. You might well need documentation of the evaluation to secure services or accommodations. And it should be clear, nontechnical, and accurate.

If you haven't received a report in a timely manner, generally around three or four weeks, call the provider and bug him until it arrives. If you feel that it contains inaccuracies or that it is unclear, contact him again and request a revised report. You're paying for the service, so make sure you get it.

Here's a sample report that might give you a flavor of what we consider to be reasonable written feedback. You'll notice that our reports are really just simple letters. They aren't especially fancy or technical-looking. Frankly, many of our colleagues worry that, if they state their results too informally or briefly, their patients won't consider the information worthwhile or authoritative. We see it differently and operate on the assumption that people respect clarity and bottom lines.

Dear Mr. Hartman:

I am writing to reiterate briefly the findings of your ADD evaluation conducted on April 12, 1994. As you know, this assessment included interviews with you and your parents, in various combinations. You also were administered a brief IQ test and standardized measures of attention and self-control. Your parents provided me with an unusually complete set of academic records, dating back to kindergarten, which included report cards and some scores from achievement tests. Finally, all of you, as well as your girlfriend, Rose, filled out symptom checklists and history forms.

As we discussed during the feedback session in my office, the diagnosis for ADD in adulthood attempts to document: (1) serious problems with impulsiveness and inattention early in life; and (2) that those same problems persist into adulthood and severely impair the person's ability to adjust.

In your case, there is clear evidence that, while your behavior did not create severe problems when you were younger, you did indeed experience difficulties concentrating, completing work successfully, and exerting self-control. Your grades were also strikingly inconsistent over time and across subjects. According to your parents and to teacher reports, you tended to start off a class highly motivated to work, experience some success in your efforts, then lose steam well before one would expect for someone of your abilities and desire to please.

Adults around you during those years did not consider you to be either hostile or defiant. They were more impressed by how much you had to struggle to accomplish simple activities, not because you were uninterested or incapable, but because of your serious problems organizing yourself and sticking with tasks until they were finished.

As for your current situation, evidence abounds that you have ongoing problems with concentration and organization. Even though you have taken yourself off athletic teams and restricted social activities in order to minimize distractions, you still struggle in an academic environment that, given your motivation and intellectual abilities, you should be able to manage easily.

All of the ratings of your behavior, whether by you, by your parents, or by Rose, describe you as an individual who often shifts from task to task. You are also uniformly characterized as having difficulty waiting, attending to conversations, managing time, and staying organized. Your legendary impatience has affected your driving record as well as your ability to manage money and other routine daily activities.

Your scores on the computerized tests were generally within normal ranges. However, according to your own ratings, you expended a great deal of effort to keep your mind from wandering. You might also remember that you developed a headache shortly after you completed the tasks.

Overall, I think there is sufficient evidence from both your past history and from your current functioning to justify a diagnosis of Attention Deficit Disorder. Essentially, you have shown long-standing difficulties with attention and self-control. They have become more pronounced over time as demands for concentration and organization have increased. In addition, there is nothing either from your history or from your current situation that can better account for this level of underachievement. While you admit to occasional bouts of mild depression, it seems that these episodes are closely tied to the frustrations you have experienced over the past few years. There is also no evidence of significant family problems or interpersonal difficulties that would account for your chronic problems with attention and self-control.

Because we discussed treatment recommendations in some detail in my office, I will reiterate them only briefly here:

1. Seek out academic assistance at your community college as soon as possible. I would first look for help in assessing your aptitude, both intellectual and vocational, so that you can make appropriate plans for your future. While you certainly have many strengths intellectually, it may well be that you are particularly good in some areas and not as strong in others. It would

be helpful for you to have some sense of your own pattern of skills.

2. You should also pursue resources available at your college that might help you better cope with the academic challenges ahead of you. It turns out that your school has an academic assistance program that offers note-taking services, tutors, and counseling. I spoke with Mr. Josephs, the head of that program, who described a host of services. He will be happy to meet with you. If you have difficulty securing either the assessment or educational services that I have described here, please feel free to contact me so that we can pursue other avenues. You might also want to be in touch with the Central Valley Learning Disabilities Association to see what they may have to offer.

3. Because of the extent to which you are encountering frustrations in your education, you should consider a trial of stimulant medication. While the use of medication will by no means remove the need for you to take responsibility for yourself and to seek supportive services, you may well find that it would help you concentrate and make better decisions. I understand that you and your parents will be contacting Dr. Stahl regarding a prescription, but, again, you should contact me if you have questions or require other referrals.

4. While you don't describe yourself as inordinately depressed or anxious, you acknowledge a constant sense of frustration and apprehension. While the medication and

academic support might help lessen some of those feelings, counseling may be in order if they persist. All the frustrations you've experienced over the years have surely taken their toll and, perhaps, should at some point be addressed. You can call me if you would like a referral for psychotherapy.

I very much enjoyed meeting with you and your parents. Let me know if I can be of any further service.

What happens if the clinician says I don't have ADD?

It's certainly possible that the clinician will make the case that you don't have ADD. Yes, you might actually hear that you're far more normal than otherwise. If you had convinced yourself that the ADD diagnosis fit you perfectly, an opinion to the contrary can be jarring.

If the clinician has conducted a full evaluation and provides compelling evidence that your concerns are unwarranted, there's not much left for you to do but accept the judgment and move on. It's really not tragic to find out that you're normal.

We've got to be candid here: Our toughest feedback interviews are those in which we have to tell people they don't have ADD. We've gotten everything from rage reactions to threatening phone calls from lawyers.

What's painful is when people hang on to the ADD label because they simply can't come to terms with their personal strengths and weaknesses. Some folks are bound and determined to see themselves as victims.

Others find it easier to claim they suffer from a disorder than to accept responsibility for poor judgment or insufficient talents.

You might also hear from the clinician that you've got identifiable problems, but of a kind separate from ADD. You can enter an evaluation thinking you have ADD and exit having learned instead that you're severely depressed or that you're an alcoholic. For many, it's easier to accept that you've got this more neutral, medical-sounding ADD problem than a more serious-sounding psychiatric syndrome. Alas, you don't have much choice but to pursue treatment for what you've got, not for what comes across as less threatening.

Principle 7

Having ADD stinks!

So much for the classiness of this book, but we seriously need to make a point here. Reading some of the popular books on ADD and listening to experts on TV, you'd get the impression that having this disorder is a wonderful blessing bestowed upon the chosen by gods above. We read how ADD makes you more creative, energetic, and spontaneous. It's also supposed to be adaptive, especially if you're into hunting and gathering.

We're sorry, but having ADD is no fun. We've dealt with hundreds of individuals with ADD over the years and, trust us, they'd rather be a little less affected by ADD and a lot more normal. You wouldn't find one of them who'd boast of having ADD or who'd characterize his problem as much of a blessing.

It's just not exhilarating always wondering if you've just screwed up or if you're about to screw up or if one of your past screwups will soon come back to haunt you. Being the family's black sheep or Bart Simpson or monumental goof-off isn't a terribly appealing role either.

It's not encouraging to be the only one in your family to have a police record or to have dropped out of school or to have gone into treatment for substance abuse. It doesn't raise your self-esteem to know that you're the one at the family picnic about whom people say, "Geez, he's the smartest one of Bob and Rose's kids, but has he ever had problems getting his act together." You probably wouldn't want to brag about having been demoted at your job because you were so hopelessly disorganized. Toiling 10 hours to accomplish what everyone else at work can do in 6 also doesn't fall into the category of "peak experience."

It doesn't surprise any of us who work in this field that "Adults with ADD" are often also "Adults with Anxiety and Depression" or "Adults with Relationship Problems" or "Adults with Drug and Alcohol Dependence." Whatever benefits one might derive from having a disinhibited style tend to be dwarfed by the disadvantages. We also haven't seen hard evidence that adults with ADD are any more creative, on the whole, than non-ADD individuals.

We have the feeling that most people who trumpet the virtues of having ADD define the disorder differently than we do. They seem to see a little ADD in everyone. For them, ADD represents a type of personality or intellectual style. From our point of view, what they're championing is the potential benefits of certain personality traits.

As you've read, we feel strongly that ADD should be reserved for characterizing individuals who experience significant impairments in their capacity to adjust both socially and in the workplace. Universalizing and glorifying these symptoms trivializes the pain experienced by adults who truly have "ADD the Disorder" as opposed to an "ADD the Character Traits."

No, we're not saying that having ADD is a ticket to unremitting misery. And not everyone with ADD is a walking poster child for one affliction or another. People can certainly compensate enough so that life can be satisfying and more. As a matter of fact, some ADD adults compensate so well that the ADD label, while perhaps technically appropriate, isn't all that relevant or useful. We'd even argue that, if you have ADD but are well-adjusted, it doesn't make much sense to still think of yourself as having ADD. ADD is a disorder, not a healthy identity.

We also acknowledge that some characteristics of ADD can be assets in certain circumstances. Spontaneity and exuberance can be benefits to salespeople, artists, and teachers alike. Many people, especially those who obsess too much before launching a project or activity, could stand to be a little less inhibited. Having a poor memory can even be helpful because you don't rely as much as on past approaches and, instead, orient yourself more toward developing novel solutions. A bad memory also has the advantage of allowing you to forget unpleasant events.

Almost any disadvantage, in some circumstances, can be an asset. The jockey's extremely short stature is also his meal ticket. In some societies schizophrenics, with their capacity for visions and otherworldliness, are assigned the role of shaman or wise man. Similar arguments can be made for every other human quality when it sits at the extreme end of a continuum.

So we understand that ADD is a problem that can be overcome and, under the right circumstances, even turned to an advantage. We just want to warn you against the romanticization of ADD as if it were an unassailable plus. Having ADD stinks. If you think you have ADD and it doesn't stink, in our book you likely don't have ADD. You might instead suffer from "Normal Human Limitations Disorder."

Principle 8

Don't be fooled by claims of magic cures for ADD.

Our comments regarding the treatment of ADD are based on certain hard-headed assumptions that you might as well know about now:

▶ ADD is a chronic condition that can be managed but not cured.

▶ ADD adults have precious little time, energy, and money to expend pursuing treatments that will likely be ineffective.

▶ You should only consider treatment programs that have withstood at least some scientific evaluation.

▶ Most successful programs for treating ADD combine medical and nonmedical interventions.

▶ The best nonmedical interventions are practical, commonsense adjustments to an impulsive and disorganized style.

We'll fill in the colors and shapes of the treatment picture over the next few sections. But first we want to make absolutely certain that we communicate how important it is for you to be wary when you hear about yet another miracle cure for ADD. Simply put, there are no cures or quick fixes. Anyone who claims to have such a remedy is misleading you.

We're more than a little alarmed by all the "cures" that are constantly being offered for ADD. It's not that we think they're necessarily proposed in bad faith. Usually it's with too much faith and not enough formal evaluation. From our standpoint, if a treatment program hasn't been verified scientifically, it shouldn't be offered, except in cases where all else has failed. Individuals with ADD suffer enough without having to spend their time and money chasing smoke.

How do I evaluate a treatment?

If someone suggests a treatment program that seems off the beaten track, ask the question, "What scientific evidence is there that this therapy works for people with my problem?" The clinician should be able to show you studies in which investigators have compared this new treatment to other treatments or to no treatment at all. You should be able to read reviews of efforts to validate the approach.

As soon as you hear the sentence, "There are no scientific studies yet, but I know this works," step away. In this day and age, it is simply unacceptable to justify treatments based upon personal belief or blind faith, especially when more rigorously tested therapies are available. No amount of testimonial, anecdote, professional opinion, advertising, or aggressive promotion can substitute for hard data concerning a treatment's effectiveness.

Advocates of nontraditional treatment approaches come up with all kinds of excuses for not testing their therapies. One common cop-out: "This treatment is so important and so obviously effective that it would be wrong to take the time to study it scientifically. Trust me, it works." Trust us, it probably doesn't.

Another cheap rationalization: "We would like to test our therapy, but we can't get federal funding because we're not in the mainstream." Well, most research is funded by sources other than the federal government. While research can be a frustrating and arduous task, anyone in a position to develop a treatment program is also in a position to encourage scientific research of its worthiness.

Aren't you being a tad rigid about the need for proof that a treatment works?

Now we can just hear you urging us to step down from our high horses. "Your insistence on scientific validation is noble but unrealistic. Everyone knows that research studies never produce clear-cut conclusions. So why bother?"

Sure, in some areas, for every study that shows a treatment works there's at least one that reaches the opposite finding. But in the course of repeated investigations, a consensus usually emerges about a therapy's potential benefits. Ultimately we all get a sense of when the treatment tends to perform well, when it doesn't, and how it's best applied.

Even if you can't collect convincing data about whether and how a treatment works, at least you can document potential side effects. It's one thing for a treatment to be of questionable utility. It's another for it to kill you.

We would also remind you of what usually happens to therapies of all kinds that are promoted with great fanfare yet little research. They usually are touted as remarkable cures one year and then show up on *20/20* or *60 Minutes* several years later to be repudiated. Think back to facilitated communication for autistic children or neurolinguistic programming for learning and emotional problems. We'll remind you again: How about all that oat bran and fish we ate thinking (wrongly) that it would lower our cholesterol? Or the fish oil we tolerated because it would make us smarter or the alar on apples we avoided because it supposedly caused cancer or the antioxidants we ingested to avoid cancer?

Many glorious cures wilt under the glare of empirical scrutiny. And, of course, some emerge with proven efficacy. Others are revised and improved. Some are administered in the same ways, but are promoted with more modest claims.

Finally, remembering that ADD is a chronic, at least partially innate, "hard-wired" condition always serves as a reference point for making judgments about which treatments might be sensible. There is no way that a five-week school training program is going to vanquish the ADD demons. Nor could you convince us that a 10-week tutoring program alone will relieve the symptoms. The impulsiveness of an ADD adult is too deeply ingrained to be erased so easily.

The symptoms of chronic conditions are resilient, persistent, and hard to cure. We should direct our efforts toward managing them over time rather than eradicating them instantly. What works at one point may need to be modified at another as new problems crop up while others diminish.

"Wait a minute!" you shout. "Didn't you carry on before about how almost no solid scientific information is available about anything related to Adult ADD? By your standards, I should be wary of anything my doctor recommends for ADD!"

You got it. With the possible exception of stimulant medication, anything beyond obvious suggestions for exerting self-control, getting organized, and exploring ways of becoming more interpersonally adept will likely fall into the "experimental" category. We're not saying to run from your doctor's suggestions. Just be aware that, at this point, justification for many of our recommendations comes more from intuition and appeals to common sense than from formal proof.

What are some of the therapies that have been explored?

Having given fair warning about the perils of untested therapies, we'd like to present the range of treatment options available and our sense of their general usefulness. It's a testament to ADD's prevalence and popularity that so many individuals from so many disciplines have offered so many treatment strategies.

The range of treatments that have been presented over the years is remarkably broad, from diets, to lighting schemes, to every medication you can think of, to herbal remedies, to prayer services. Some can work, some sure looked like they'd work but don't, others seemed nuts from the outset, and others fall into the category of "Doesn't sound right but you never know." The broad range of treatments also reflects societal interests (diet therapies) and regional preferences (megavitamins in California, oil of early evening primrose in England, and inner ear treatments on the noisy East Coast).

The wide spectrum of treatments falls into various categories of legitimacy. The first group, listed below, are those remedies that have been disproved or chronically untested (which we always assume means that their proponents are afraid to find out their treatment might not work).

Our purpose in presenting this list is not to deride efforts to find a better way. Many if not all of these approaches were pursued in good faith and perhaps for what seemed at the time to be solid theoretical justification. There's just no evidence at this time that they are generally worthwhile for the treatment of ADD.

- ▶ Removal of dietary sugar
- ▶ Removal of food additives, dyes, etc.
- ▶ Megavitamin therapy
- ▶ Herbal remedies/folk cures
- ▶ Efamol food supplements
- ▶ Caffeine

- ► Removal of fluorescent lights
- ► Sensory motor integration
- ► Biofeedback training/relaxation exercises
- ► Treatment for inner ear disturbances
- ► Vision training
- ► Chiropractic manipulations

The most controversial unproven cure at the moment is EEG biofeedback. Proponents are marketing it aggressively despite the absence of credible data to support its effectiveness. While at some point a controlled trial may prove it worthwhile, none have been published in scientific journals. Given its expense and dubious benefit, we are loath to suggest it to our patients of any age.

Despite all the recent press regarding sugar's innocence in causing behavior problems, diet as demon still holds strong sway over the public's minds. While we are sure that there are children whose behavior is drastically affected by foods, we've never seen any in our offices. We've heard parents claim that their children goes berserk with a brownie, but in all instances the child went berserk regularly without dessert.

If a parent claims that controlling the diet makes a difference, we'll rarely intervene, operating on the assumption that children can survive without sweets. We've also always believed that putting a child on a diet involves what can be a positive imposition of structure. It may also give parents a greater sense of having some control and doing something positive for their child.

Several recent academic articles document these sorts of secondary psychological effects of dietary regimen.

So which approaches will most likely work?

The strategy most likely to work for most with ADD combines medication with common sense, systematic efforts at lifestyle adjustments. We'll detail both components of this strategy over the remainder of this book. You'll read about the potential benefits and limits of medication. We'll also try to convey the crucial importance of adopting a problem-solving spirit.

As we've mentioned repeatedly, our patients and audiences are often disappointed that we don't have magic answers to offer. Understandably, they're looking for elaborate programs and surefire remedies. We're afraid that most of the enduring help you'll secure will come more from medication and gradual adjustments than from instant cures.

Principle 9

Medication: The stuff usually works.

ADD is a good news/bad news disorder. The bad news you've heard about: It's not always easy to identify or document. The good news is that there's a generally safe and easily administered treatment that can often produce marked improvement. Indeed, it is so effective that it works not only for ADD, but also for enhancing performance in people with many other disorders and even with no disorders at all.

The treatment we're talking about, of course, is stimulant medication. Medicines like Ritalin and Dexedrine, when taken in low to moderate doses, usually improve a human's ability to concentrate and to exert self-control.

Notice we didn't limit the description of stimulant effects just to people with ADD. The drugs have the same sort of impact on nearly everyone, except perhaps for individuals who are psychotic or out-of-control anxious. You might not think that a class of medications termed *stimulants* would actually have a calming effect, but that's exactly what they do for almost everyone.

How can stimulants create healthy restraint? Because what they're stimulating are the parts of the brain whose function it is to put the brakes on. At the doses these medications are prescribed, they increase the brain's ability to stop behavior.

With the brain more poised to inhibit, an individual is in a better position to stop and consider consequences before rushing to action. He is also more likely to keep from responding to events that are irrelevant to the task at hand. Enhanced self-control and concentration can greatly improve productivity and adjustment, especially if you are by nature unusually impulsive and inattentive.

Literally hundreds of well-controlled studies have explored the impact of stimulants on ADD symptoms. While almost all these investigations have involved children and adolescents, several have shown similar results with adults. Regardless of your philosophical stance regarding the use of medication, it's hard to look at this mountain of research data and see anything other than clear evidence documenting the effectiveness and relative safety of stimulant therapy. The stuff usually works and with generally little down-side.

How well do these medications work?

Here we go with another answer that starts with "It depends . . ." But, yes, it depends on how severe the symptoms are, on what kinds of other problems might coexist with the ADD, and on the person's biological makeup. In children, the conservative figure for drug response is somewhere between 70 and 80 percent.

Most youngsters are better able to attend and to sit still while they are on the medication.

Notice we stuck in the phrase "while they are on the medication." That's the reality. Stimulants, just like aspirin, don't permanently change anything. They do their thing, get chemically digested, and exit.

The picture with adults, as always, is less clear. Based on the few controlled studies available, it looks as if the rate of positive medication response falls somewhere between 60 and 70 percent. At least that's the current estimate we're all spouting.

Although that's not a bad hit rate, most of us in the field suspect that it will rise as diagnostic criteria tighten. Why? Because the medication will most help those who most need it. If your study includes people who aren't terribly impaired, there's not as much room for improvement. Those subjects are close to normal anyway.

Having near-normal people in a drug study messes up the chances of showing statistical change. So does having people incorrectly classified as having ADD, particularly if those people are mostly emotionally disturbed and therefore not as likely to respond well. As our technical ability to get clean groups of ADD subjects improves, you'll likely see rates of positive drug response climb at least to the 70 to 80 percent range, if not higher.

How can two psychologists who have such an obvious penchant for obsessing about scientific niceties be so sure? Because we've seen what's happened in the child arena. Estimates for drug response have steadily risen as diagnostic techniques have improved. As a matter of fact, some recent studies of very carefully selected ADD children have shown response rates upwards of 90 percent.

Does this mean that stimulants will necessarily work for you? If someone has symptoms serious enough to warrant a diagnosis of ADD, the chances are pretty decent. People with profound problems concentrating and getting organized usually find that the medicine helps. But "pretty decent" and "usually" aren't the same as "100 percent" and "always." You never know until you try.

Fortunately, the stimulants are easy medications to experiment with because they have an almost immediate effect as well as a quick departure. That means you don't have to wait weeks for the drug to build up in the bloodstream to see if you respond. Some can detect an impact just 30 minutes or so after taking a dose. And, if there is a problem, you don't have to wait weeks for it to leave your system. All of this makes for relatively simple adjustments in the amount and timing of drug administrations.

While we've indicated that medications for ADD can help many with the disorder, we don't want to convey the impression that they will chemically remove every ounce of distress. As you'll read shortly, medications don't cure all symptoms, even when they work dramatically well. While they might reduce those symptoms directly tied to impulsiveness and inattention, they usually don't address directly or rapidly those tagalong problems we described in "Principle 5: ADD is a disorder that loves company."

Stimulants also won't undo those deeply ingrained bad habits you might have developed around dealing with others or in viewing the world as unfair or depressing. While experiencing the greater success medications can promote might eventually improve your mood and coping, time and other interventions usually must be part of the mix. We'll be driving this point home throughout the rest of this book.

How do you decide whether or not to take the medication?

The decision to take medication is a highly personal one and should be approached as such. Even if your husband or wife stands in front of you with a bottle of Ritalin in one hand and a divorce decree in the other and says, "Choose!" don't leap until you're ready. Medication trials will often fail when patients don't feel fully informed and at least marginally comfortable with the decision. This is why we've emphasized the importance of working with a clinician who can respond to your questions and concerns.

So don't feel that getting a diagnosis of ADD means you should lunge immediately at every pill bottle that comes your way. If you've waited this long to start medication, you might as well hold off until you're sure it makes sense. People will stay on medications they feel informed about and comfortable taking.

Here are some general guidelines for deciding about medication:

▶ You have a lifelong history of impulsiveness

Principle 9 115

and inattention that continues to significantly hamper your ability to function at home and at work.

▶ You've spent a lifetime trying to compensate for those symptoms and it's just not working for you anymore.

▶ Bad things (like academic, job, and relationship failure) are happening or about to happen and you can't afford to mess up any longer.

▶ Frustrations around poor organization and its impact are so intense that you're extremely upset, panicky, and otherwise beside yourself.

We're sure it's not lost on you that the guidelines for deciding about taking medication are also the guidelines for making the ADD diagnosis to begin with. The assigning of that label indicates problems serious enough to warrant a trial of medication. The implication? Get a good evaluation before you try ADD-improving drugs. If that evaluation points to ADD, a stab at medication is frequently a sensible step.

How often do you have to take the medication?

Most school-aged ADD children take two or three doses of stimulants per day because their schedule usually never lets up on pressures for attention and organization. Whether it's getting books together in the morning or sitting through hours of classes or buckling down to do homework and practicing, children are forever confronted with demands to stay focused and organized.

Children also haven't had much chance yet to find a niche that helps them avoid situations bound to cause them grief. Kids can't take exciting jobs that involve running about or collaboration with a team of other, perhaps more organized, coworkers. They have to sit in earth science class whether or not they like it or find it easy.

Adults often have schedules with more discrete demands for attention. They are apt to take medication more on an "as needed basis." One of our patients, a manager at a car dealership, takes just one pill in the morning. This is when he needs to complete various sales reports and tracking forms. Since he spends the rest of the day bounding around the lot, he feels he can do without an afternoon dose of the medication.

College students will also tailor their medication schedule to meet academic demands. Because their classes are often organized in blocks that fall on two or three days of the week, they might take the medication regularly during these "peak" times and then again only when necessary. For example, they might take a pill during specific study hours or when gearing up for exams or a project.

Remember that patients who are prescribed stimulant medication undergo a process of experimentation. Along with their doctor, they learn what doses are most effective, how long the benefits tend to last, and how best to time them to maximize their impact. As we've mentioned, the way stimulants behave makes that process relatively easy.

Predictably, problems with medication stem more from human nature than from the mysteries of neurochemistry. Patients frequently are uninformed or ill-advised about how to take the medication. Some think that it must be ingested at rigid time intervals (maybe every four hours) or only before noon. Others have been told that drug "holidays" of several weeks' duration are required every three or four months.

Perhaps one of the biggest errors comes from people calculating maximum doses based on how much medication they take during the entire day rather than at any specific administration. The way most of the stimulants act, especially the standard formulations as opposed to the longer-acting ones, calculating a daily dose is irrelevant because the drug doesn't build up in the bloodstream over the course of a day. Each dose fades at the end of a few hours and has little if any impact on the next round.

How about the longer-acting stimulants?

Some of the longer-acting stimulants, like Sustained-Release Ritalin and the Dexedrine Spansules, are designed to spread the medication out so you don't need to keep taking them constantly. They're especially helpful for people who need medication throughout the day but forget to take it.

While the longer-acting stimulants can work well, we usually recommend at least starting with the standard, quick-acting brand so you can get a feel for the medication's impact and possible side effects. If you then are confident about the effects, you can try moving on to the sustained-release formulations.

Just remember that 20 milligrams dispensed into the bloodstream over six to eight hours will provide less medication at any one point than the 20 milligrams that worked over two or three hours. We mention this because we've met patients who were doing fine on 20 milligrams of the standard formulation and then shifted over to 20 milligrams of the longer-acting medication only to report that it didn't work as well. It's because the switchover actually decreased the amount of stimulants in the bloodstream at any given time. This is why it's not at all unusual for patients taking the longer-acting medication to also take "booster" doses of the regular brew when demands for attention are the highest.

The watchwords for this entire process are "common sense." If at 6:30 A.M. you take a medication that's effective for only three hours, it's not going to help you much if most demands on your attention occur after lunch (unless of course you take a lunchtime dose). It also isn't necessarily sensible to restrict doses to the daytime if your evenings are filled with endless responsibilities for concentration and planning.

How will I know it works for me?

Most of our patients have the notion that you take this little pill and cataclysmic events promptly ensue. If they've watched *Geraldo* recently, they're waiting to shrink three feet, lock into a zombie stare, and reach for an axe in prelude to perpetrating a series of grisly murders.

Sorry, but it's not that sensational (or destructive). While the ultimate impact can be dramatic, the moment-to-moment effects are subtle. Most of our patients don't feel much different at all, and they certainly don't experience gross changes in personality or mood.

If they notice anything, it's usually more on the order of grace notes than symphonies. They'll see that their handwriting improves or that they're more apt to think before acting on an impulse. After a few days they might realize that they've been better able to focus in a class or on a project. These nuances in behavior taken individually might not seem like much initially, but they can combine to produce some major changes.

It's best to judge the effects of medication while you're in situations requiring attention. If you first take it during a vacation, you might not see effects. It would be better to try it during times in which your problems with attention and disorganization are most likely to surface.

In most cases, drug effects are monitored informally between patient and doctor. People take it and simply see if it makes a difference. But the impact of medication can be monitored more formally. The most sophisticated approach entails repeating, at different dose levels, the rating scales that were administered during the initial evaluation. You then can judge whether higher doses of the drugs measurably improve those ratings. While this strategy for adjusting medication is ideal, it's usually not pursued because of the time and effort involved.

Even though the drug has a relatively immediate neurological effect, it's best to judge its general impact over at least a few weeks. When you first take medication, you'll focus on your behavior much more closely than ever before because you'll be trying to determine if the pills help. People sometimes think that they're behaving differently (for the good or otherwise) when, in fact, they have always been that way but just hadn't noticed it.

Here's an example: A young man started taking Ritalin following a thorough evaluation. Several days after the first dose he called greatly concerned that he had developed a twitch in his eye as a result of the medication. He was very worried that the medication had caused permanent brain damage.

Because the fellow had undergone a comprehensive assessment, the psychiatrist treating him had information about his predrug condition. On those baseline rating scales, both his parents and girlfriend had indicated that the patient had the habit of twitching his eyes, especially when he was tired. When these same people were asked to rate his twitching now that he was on medication, their responses indicated that there had been no changes.

What are the side effects?

The side effects of the stimulants tend to be temporary and mild, but you should know about them in some detail. Before we list the most common, be aware of the following:

▶ While the typical side effects of medication are

well documented, you never know how you will respond until you try it. Medication response is like a fingerprint: Everybody's got one, but each is unique.

▶ The higher the dose you take, the more likely you'll experience a side effect.

▶ Make sure the physician knows about any medical problems or undiagnosed symptoms you might have. Be especially open about any problems you may have had involving your heart and lungs. Stimulant medications can raise your blood pressure. If you already have high blood pressure, your physician should monitor you carefully.

▶ If you do experience a side effect that bothers you, call the prescribing physician and tell him about it. It's better to check it out than to sit back and worry that you're literally about to check out.

▶ Unless the side effect is severe or seems as if it could get serious, you shouldn't stop taking the medication altogether without consulting the physician. We make a point of this because too often patients, especially those who haven't been well informed, experience a mild side effect and abruptly stop taking the medicine (sometimes never to return to the doctor).

Here are the "typical" side effects of methylphenidate (Ritalin) and Dexedrine:

▶ Diminished appetite while on the medication.

▶ Trouble falling asleep (especially if a late afternoon dose is administered).

► Edginess or irritability at the end of the dose period. This is called "rebound effect" and is usually controlled by adjustments in the size and timing of doses.

We put the "typical" in quotation marks to emphasize that, while they're the most frequent, these side effects are neither common nor uniform. For example, we've dealt with many patients, both young and old, who sleep *better* with a late afternoon dose of medication. We'd love to give you the percentage of Ritalin users who experience each type of side effect, but that information has yet to be gathered scientifically.

And now for some side effects you'll hardly ever (or never) experience. If you even think that the medication is causing one of the following, reach for the phone and call your physician:

► Major alterations in personality
► Diminished athletic ability
► Decreased creativity
► Physical addiction

In the next section, we'll talk about some curious psychological side effects of getting better. It shakes people up that they can change so dramatically by taking this innocuous-looking little pill. Change, even when it's for the better, is almost always hard on people. Almost as hard as remaining unchanged.

If the stuff is so safe and effective, why all the fuss?

The debate regarding the use of biological treatments for ADD hasn't been so much: "Does it work?" as it has been: "Is it right to do?" These ethical issues have erupted most often around the treatment of ADD in children. Many have raised questions about the appropriateness of using drugs to control a child's behavior.

We're getting the impression that the use of these medications isn't quite as controversial in adults, probably because older patients have more say in the decision. With children, the push for medication comes from the adults. Children aren't in a position to exercise free choice.

Youngsters aren't known for walking into a doctor's office saying, "Sir, I seem to be having chronic problems with inhibition and sustained attention that are truly interfering with my overall functioning. What do you think about a trial of a psychostimulant?" More often they experience some combination of bewilderment, humiliation, frustration, and rage, none of which is lessened by a process that too often treats them more as specimens than as players.

Adults, of course, can take a more active role in decisions to seek evaluation and treatment. By this point in their life, they have an extensive track record that can be reviewed and judged. Also, they often have exhausted most of their nonmedical options and are looking to take the next step.

So, ironically, the question we're hearing more nowadays isn't "How can you even think of prescribing these drugs?" Instead we're asked, "What's wrong with taking stimulants whether you're ADD or not? If this medication is effective, safe, and improves performance, why not put it in the water supply or at least spray it on the Wheaties?"

We've always found it hard to respond to this question without sounding like puritan preachers lecturing on the importance of independence, personal responsibility, and hard work. Fact is, the answer falls more in the realm of the philosophical than the clinical.

Our society generally feels that medical treatments should be reserved for the truly impaired. For example, growth hormone not only makes unusually short children taller, but it also can increase the stature of youngsters whose height falls in the normal range. Nonetheless, most would frown on injecting average-height children with growth hormone.

This issue of using performance-enhancing drugs even if you're not flat out abnormal grows ever larger with the release of each new psychoactive medication. The popular book *Listening to Prozac* by Dr. Peter Kramer grapples with the ethical concerns brought about by wide-scale use of the new-wave antidepressants. You could easily substitute Ritalin for Prozac in the title and confront the same ethical issues.

These grand moral quandaries aside, we have seen instances where medication has made matters worse, even in the absence of formal side effects. Here's a listing of some actual scenarios:

- ▶ College student decides recent low grades in the premed courses result from ADD rather than from lower aptitude in the sciences. Pursues evaluations and medication rather than reconsideration of career choice.

- ▶ Overly aggressive and generally obnoxious businessman decides that ADD led to his being fired. Wouldn't hear of counseling, but found a physician willing to prescribe stimulants. Although he's somewhat more organized, he's still overly aggressive and generally obnoxious.

- ▶ Adolescent convinces parents that he has ADD even though he's far more antisocial than impulsive or inattentive. Parents talk pediatrician into prescribing stimulants, which the youngster promptly starts selling to classmates for them to smoke and snort.

While we've tried to allay any unfounded fears you might have about taking medication, we don't intend to be glib about it either. Taking medication is serious business and should be approached as such.

Why aren't you talking much about medications other than the stimulants?

Because we don't have much solid information to report on nonstimulant therapies. Whenever a new disorder gets "discovered," medications of every shape and size are thrown at it, sometimes with a theoretical rationale and other times simply to see what will happen. Out of this process can evolve important discoveries and new therapies.

Unfortunately, that process hasn't played itself out yet for ADD in adults. We're still at the "maybe this will work" stage. You'll be hearing media reports and other descriptions of various medications undergoing evaluation. Some will pan out, and others, of course, will fade in popularity.

This is what we do know: For most ADD adults, stimulants are the treatment of choice because they are safe and proven effective. In most cases, they should be tried first because they offer the greatest chance of benefit and the fewest side effects.

If someone responds poorly or not at all to the stimulants, he has other options. The next line of attack would involve the use of antidepressants. Antidepressants have certain appeal. First, they are longer acting so you don't have to keeping taking pills every few hours. Second, they often elevate one's mood. Given that so many patients with Adult ADD are unhappy, this would seem to be a nice extra benefit.

A side comment: In our experience, mood elevation isn't the sole province of the antidepressants. Indeed, there is some evidence that stimulants can also relieve symptoms of depression, but perhaps for different reasons. Antidepressants affect how the mood centers of the brain function. Stimulants may improve mood less directly by allowing for greater accomplishment. Simply put, you can shed pounds of unhappiness and self-loathing by experiencing success.

The antidepressants that are used for the treatment of Adult ADD generally fall into two classes: tricyclic antidepressants (TCAs for short) and selective serotonin reuptake inhibitors (SSRIs). The TCAs include medications such as imipramine (the brand name is Tofranil) and desipramine (Norpramine). Although they have been shown effective in treating ADD in children, they aren't typically as helpful as the stimulants. We're not aware of any formal studies of their usefulness in treating adults. We do know that practitioners will rely on TCAs when patients can't take stimulants (usually because of tics or Tourette's syndrome) or haven't responded well to them.

While TCAs might be a reasonable alternative, keep in mind that they are far less safe than the stimulants. The chances of side effects or of becoming seriously ill are much higher with the TCAs than with the stimulants. If you are placed on a TCA, you should expect to undergo regular medical evaluations to ensure that the various blood levels and indicators of heart functioning are normal.

We're not saying that taking TCAs will surely kill you. They can be and often are managed safely and with good result. We just want to make sure you realize that they can't be handled at the same comfort level as the stimulants. To our constant dismay, some physicians deal with stimulants and antidepressants as if they were equally safe. But they're not.

The second class of antidepressants you might encounter, SSRIs, will sound more familiar to you because it includes medications such as fluoxetine (Prozac). Although SSRIs are prescribed for ADD, no scientific studies of their effectiveness have been published regarding children or adults. They do have some possible advantages over the TCAs because they're safer (although still not as safe as the stimulants) and easier to monitor. They might also be better for ADD patients who are seriously depressed or have symptoms of obsessive-compulsive disorder.

Our general recommendation is to start, if at all possible, with what's known to be safe and effective before moving on to alternatives. If your physician chooses medications other than the stimulants, make sure he has a sound reason. The same goes for combinations of medication, let's say Ritalin and Prozac. These blends might be appropriate, but only with solid justification and careful trials.

Any word on which ADD-related drugs don't mix well with other drugs or substances?

All current indications are that the stimulants are generally safe, even in combination with most other medications or substances such as tobacco, alcohol, or caffeine. While stimulants might slightly enhance or minimize the effects of these other substances, there's no evidence of dangerous interactions. Even if you take an overdose of a stimulant (which we definitely don't recommend), it probably won't kill you. We haven't seen any evidence that people have died or suffered permanent physical damage from taking this class of medications.

While it is true that stimulants can, in a small percentage of people who take them, raise blood pressure, this isn't usually a serious concern. The stimulants generally have about the same heart effects as over-the-counter decongestants. Again, there is no evidence that the stimulants cause high blood pressure that produces strokes or heart attacks.

Before placing you on medication, your physician will certainly take your blood pressure to make sure you don't have a previously undetected heart ailment. If you already are being treated for high blood pressure, you should be especially diligent about attending your routine follow-up appointments. Your doctor might make some adjustments in your blood pressure medication if you're taking a stimulant.

As we just mentioned in the previous section, the antidepressants are not as safe as the stimulants. An overdose of a TCA is often lethal. You also need to be more careful about potential drug interactions, although these medications have been available for years without causing serious problems.

Even though these medications aren't normally harmful when taken at appropriate doses, let the prescribing physician know about anything you're taking that might mix poorly with them. It pays to be cautious because potential side effects have not been studied systematically in groups of ADD adults.

Do you have to stay on the medication forever?

No. Well, maybe. Our patients continue with the medication as long as they feel they need it to function adequately. If they're not sure, they stop taking the medication for awhile and see if it makes any difference. It's usually not terribly hard to tell.

Some of our patients who started taking medication in college have since stopped because they are in a work and home situation that they can manage without pharmaceutical assistance. Many others continue taking their medication on a daily basis because they have no question that their ability to handle their affairs is markedly enhanced by the therapy.

As best as anyone can tell, no health risks are associated with long-term use of stimulants. But here again we don't know for sure. The identification and treatment of Adult ADD is so new that not enough years have passed to allow for careful scientific study. Because the stimulants make such a fleeting biological appearance, most consider it unlikely that low-dose administration could lead to any enduring problems. It's just that we all won't know with any certainty for years.

What's the hardest part of taking medication?

We should end with a dose of non-Ritalin-induced reality. The hardest part of stimulant therapy for ADD isn't decisions about doses, or types of medication, or when to take them, or how to monitor the effects, or potential medical complication, or any other specific action of the drugs themselves. The greatest challenge comes in finding a physician who will write you a prescription.

As we mentioned earlier, few physicians of any breed are currently involved in ADD medication management.

People have to travel to other cities, offer their firstborn, and promise eternal salvation in order to get in the door.

Ironically, many physicians who work with ADD find it rewarding. There aren't many other areas of medicine where you can produce such an immediate and dramatic benefit at such a low cost all around. Our stimulant-prescribing colleagues regale us with heart-warming stories of people who quickly went from miserable failure to remarkable success. You can be a hero with relative ease. That's if you made the initial diagnostic call accurately, which, as you've learned, is the not so gratifying or simple part of the process.

Incidentally, we almost listed another problem as "Most likely to interfere with successful drug treatment." This one flows from the fact that medications can't work unless the patient takes them. Even miracle drugs are rendered useless when they sit in the pill bottle instead of float in the bloodstream. Remembering to take medications is a special problem for our ADD patients, who, by definition, don't handle routine tasks reliably. Those pill dispensers that beep at preset intervals must have been designed by an engineer with an ADD adult in mind.

Principle **10**

Getting better might make matters worse.

Nothin's much finer than a good fantasy. Dreams of universal adulation, vast wealth, legendary romantic prowess, and 100 percent accuracy on four-foot putts help most of us smooth the grittier surfaces of reality. Not that we have anything against reality, mind you. It's just not always as much fun or disease-free.

Patients who seek a diagnosis of ADD sometimes harbor the fantasy that a label and a pill will quickly end all suffering and begin a new age of joy. To be sure, learning you have a legitimate problem that can be treated often brings enormous relief and comfort. And, as you'll read, treatment can help most of our patients make positive changes in their lives.

But the journey to greater happiness and adjustment is more like a tumultuous sea voyage than a weekend junket to the Caribbean. Many of our patients are surprised and confused by the surge of emotions they confront upon hearing confirmation of their ADD. And if those mixed and nagging feelings aren't dealt with effectively, treatment suffers.

Frankly, we were surprised when many of our patients showed psychological side effects to getting better. We

---

naively thought that they'd be thrilled with their much-improved life circumstance, follow up on treatment, and count themselves fortunate.

We were dead wrong. For one thing, we had forgotten an elemental characteristic of human nature: that change, even for the better, is threatening, unsettling, and confusing. Stimulants may have enhanced attention and self-control, but they hadn't (and couldn't) help our patients deal with the fallout from transitions. And as we keep mentioning, medications won't erase the poor self-esteem and unproductive ways of relating to others that might have built up over the years.

When you've been the way you've been for 20 or 30 or 40 years, a sudden shift can, to use the vernacular, blow you away. You may be delighted that life's gotten better, but you start to wonder who you are if a medication can so abruptly change your fortunes. Am I still me? Is this just a cheap fix for something I should be working at much harder? Am I taking the medication just to make it easier for my wife or boss to deal with me? If I perform better, will people begin to expect too much from me? Will I become boring and bored?

To give you a few examples of what we mean, we present below unadorned accounts from our clinical experience.

Dirty Black Sneakers

Greg was an X-ray technician who, after 10 years of being nagged by family, friends, neighbors, priests, and employers, sought an evaluation for ADD. He met every criterion for the disorder you could imagine and, despite some hesitancy, began a trial of medication.

The medication had an immediate and dramatic effect on his performance. His boss went from threatening termination to offering him a supervisory position. His girlfriend couldn't get over the difference in his attentiveness to her and to his household responsibilities. Everyone was thrilled.

Everyone, that is, except for Greg. Oh, he liked the kudos he was receiving all around. But he nevertheless stopped taking the medication after only four months.

In response to his girlfriend's dire threats, Greg came in to talk about what led him to discontinue treatment. He started to explain his position and then abruptly pointed to his torn black canvas sneakers. "You see these tennis shoes?" he asked. "They're dirty, ugly, and ripped, and I probably should buy a new pair of Nikes or Adidas. But I love these old sneakers. They're comfortable and what I'm used to, faults and all."

He then drew the parallel between his old sneakers and his old (non-Ritalin) self. He may have been more appealing and productive on the medication, but it wasn't what he was used to. "It wasn't me. It was the drug, and I couldn't handle that." He also made it clear that what we were calling a disorder, he considered his personality. "What you're labeling ADD is who I am."

Greg was also was terrified that he wouldn't be able to meet the new expectations at his job and home. "There are advantages to being considered an idiot," he said, "because nobody demands much of you."

Finally, Greg didn't like at all that the medication promoted reflection about past events and future consequences. For the first time in his life he experienced daily anxiety because he considered bad things that might happen to him. As he put it so eloquently, "This thinking about stuff sucks."

The Good Samaritan

Gene was thoroughly engaging and well liked for his neighborliness. He spent most of his leisure time helping others with projects and home maintenance problems. Not many community events or groups lacked his involvement.

While he might have attended to the needs of all the neighbors, he was rarely at home. His wife and children thought he flitted about to avoid demands for more sustained effort of the sort required at home. They all worried about the debts the family was amassing because Gene wasn't careful about sending invoices out for his professional services. After they saw a segment about Adult ADD on television, his entire family got together and convinced him to seek an evaluation.

As it turned out, Gene did have ADD. But he was very resistant to the diagnosis because he prided himself on being a "Good Samaritan." He felt that people wouldn't like him anymore if he were less apt to bounce from home to home and event to event. He saw his reputation for helpfulness as his way of feeling useful and good about himself.

After starting medication, Gene became far more diligent but seriously depressed. He began to see that he had missed many chances to interact with his children. Remorse over how he had treated his wife over the years overwhelmed him. He felt sadness over his consistent absence from the home and over the flood of missed opportunities. It took many months of counseling before he could leave the past behind and adjust to his new role as an involved husband and father.

I Would If I Could

Chris was a sandy-haired, 19-year-old freshman enrolled in a small community college. Despite substantial intellectual ability, he was failing nearly all his courses. With the help of a sympathetic assistant dean, the student found his way to an ADD evaluation. That assessment verified the diagnosis and led to a trial of stimulants, to which Chris responded favorably.

The account would end here except for what newscaster Paul Harvey would call "the rest of the story." In this case the complications arose from Chris's overwhelming fury at his parents and former teachers for years of not trusting him. "I kept telling them that I would do better if I could do better, but they just said I was lazy and irresponsible. They'd lecture me endlessly, compare me unfavorably to my older sister, and generally make me feel like crap. I don't remember ever being happy through high school, and it's because they didn't believe me when I tried to explain that I couldn't pay attention like the other kids, even when I tried."

When we describe his fury as "overwhelming," we're not exaggerating. It interfered with his family relationships in that he would have nothing to do with his parents for many months. Nearly every time he took his pill and experienced its effects, he'd get indignant and bitter all over again.

Chris's parents were alternately racked with guilt or equally furious at him for laying blame at their feet. It took several intense family sessions and almost a year until the family waters cooled from boiling to a simmer.

You Can Run, but You Cannot Hide

Mary Alice, the mother of two world-class ADD boys, never had much doubt that her children came by their disorder honestly. Marriage and motherhood had provided her with safe escape from endless school failure and disappointment. Described by her husband as "raw energy," Mary Alice careened from activity to activity in a whirl of motion.

After her boys were identified and treated, Mary Alice decided it was time to take a look at herself. She was tired of being the butt of jokes and, more pointedly, of her husband's complaints about her disorganization and spaciness.

The psychologist who was treating the boys also evaluated Mary Alice. Because he had endured countless no-show appointments, after-hours phone calls, and overdue invoices, only professional ethics kept him from saying, "Don't bother with the evaluation, Mary Alice. You've got ADD as surely as the sun doth shine."

Mary Alice responded well to Dexedrine in that she was far more organized in her daily tasks. Her attention span increased enough to consider a return to school. It bothered her, though, that she still never seemed to relax and that she was more apt to worry than in years past.

At first Mary Alice chalked up her free-floating discomfort to the stress of dealing with the boys. But she became so anxious that she worried about possible medication side effects or that she was having a nervous breakdown. She returned to the psychologist.

Over several sessions Mary Alice began talking about her childhood, especially violence witnessed and abuse suffered. The following picture emerged: For years her active style allowed her to cope through motion. "As long as I kept moving I didn't need to deal with the ugliness of it all. And moving came easily to me." Now in her late thirties and focused a bit by the medication, Mary Alice had more chance to reflect and, like our patient, Greg, became agitated by emotions previously left in the dust. She couldn't truly settle herself down until she had a chance to deal with the past.

How Dare You Say I'm Better!

Although Patty had accepted her diagnosis of ADD, she adamantly resisted stimulant therapy. She had taken medication during one semester of community college and her grades improved substantially. However, she attributed this not to the medication, but to her resolve to do better. The following semester she did not take the medication and achieved relatively well, thus proving her point.

Patty now performs in local community theater and is regarded as an accomplished actress. She came in for a consultation agitated about an experience at her dress rehearsal.

Patty, having landed a major part in a play, was having difficulty remembering her lines, cues, and timing. On a whim, she took some leftover Ritalin prior to the dress rehearsal. Unfortunately (according to Patty), her timing became impeccable, her delivery crisp and precise, and her overall performance excellent.

After the show, the director ran to Patty, threw his arms around her neck, and shouted, "What happened to you! You were absolutely marvelous tonight!"

Patty was crushed. She couldn't handle that the medication so dramatically changed her performance. Was she only a good actress if she took medication? What did that say about the nature of her talents and about who she was?

We're always hesitant to talk about "typical" characteristics of ADD or "typical" reactions to treatment because we know full well that there's nothing "typical" about any single individual's behavior. People with ADD are as different from one another as the rest of us are, even though experts can give the impression that their patients are all cut from the same cloth. Show us a "typical" reaction and we'll show you a dozen folks with ADD whose experience has been just the opposite.

You've seen in the anecdotes we've just presented a range of responses. If there's any common thread we've noticed, it's that the diagnosis and treatment of ADD creates a pool of mixed emotions: relief that there's an explanation for longstanding problems, but wariness about unfamiliar therapeutic ventures. There's anticipation of new beginnings, but anger and sadness over past mistakes. Renewed confidence and energy can blend with confusion and uncertainty. A sense of vindication can run alongside feelings of grief and mourning over what might have been.

For all we know, you might be diagnosed with ADD, benefit from treatment, and have no unusual problems at all adjusting, except perhaps for how to express your happiness. It should only be. We just want you to know that sometimes it's not quite that straightforward. Change, even for the better, brings unexpected upheavals. If you know that going in, coming out successfully is easier.

Principle 11

With or without medication, life goes on.

Now for another set of our biases that you should know about up front:

▶ While stimulants are the treatment of choice for ADD, most of our patients, even those who respond positively to the medication, still must make nonmedical adjustments in their lives.

▶ Those nonmedical adjustments usually represent small tinkerings in lifestyle rather than grand programs or interventions.

▶ The most essential strategies involve finding manageable home and work environments and then tailoring them to your strengths and weaknesses.

▶ Most of the advice you get for dealing with ADD is overly complicated.

▶ Anyone, ADD or not, would benefit from the nonmedical interventions experts typically suggest. It's just that, if you're ADD, you need these strategies to survive.

How do you develop ways of compensating for ADD?

First we want to point out that you've already developed a whole range of compensations. You can't help it as, year after year, you've tried to work around your disorganization and inattention. Many of these strategies have helped while others proved useless or counterproductive. As we keep indicating, one way to justify a diagnosis of ADD is when efforts to compensate fail to bring about reasonable adjustment.

Often we see evidence of some of these strategies even before we see the patient. Our secretaries have compiled a list of "red flags":

▶ Someone other than the patient calls for the appointment.

▶ The patient calls for the appointment, but then calls back several times just to double-check the date, time, and place of the appointment.

▶ Someone else calls back to double-check the date, time and place of the appointment.

▶ The patient calls fifteen minutes after the time of the appointment to double-check the date, time, and place of the appointment.

▶ The patient calls for an appointment and then must call back because he cannot find his calendar.

▶ The patient rushes in at the appointed time and breathlessly asks if he is in the right place.

► The secretary notices an extra set of keys around the patient's neck, much like your mother made you do to make sure you didn't lose a mitten.

During our interviews with patients we hear all sorts of examples of how they have coped with their ADD symptoms by adopting different personality styles. We've listed some of the more common below.

The Wallflower: If you almost always foul up when you take action, you can learn quickly that passivity is a fine protection against failure. If you let others take the initiative, you can follow from a safe distance. Not only do you not have to take any responsibility, but you also have a built-in mechanism for controlling your impulsiveness (by doing little on your own). Of course, this means that you often have to submit to the will of others and deny your own desires. But, to some, it's worth the price.

The Clown: Adopting the role of a clown serves many masters. If you're funny, people will stick with you longer and put up with more. Most folks expect clowns to act silly and make mistakes. If you act like life's a lark, you can always hope that people think your errors flow more from lack of concern than from lack of control.

Humor also protects you from hurt and disappointment. One of our patients told us, "As long as I keep joking, I can keep from thinking about the pain I feel."

Being the clown does have its downside: People don't take you seriously even when you want them to. They also wonder if you're superficial.

The Rebel without a Clue: A surefire way to exert control and cope with confusion is to define yourself as a rebel. Can't decide what you really want? No problem. Just do the opposite of what everyone else is doing. Want to cover up for failure? Easy. Just act like you got into trouble out of your own free will. Are you finding that being angry with yourself gets you down? Hell, take the pressure off and get angry at the world. Blaming strangers beats blaming yourself.

The Overachiever: Some people deal with insults to their self-esteem through a dogged pursuit of achievement and external signs of productivity and acceptance. They protect themselves with observable signs of their worth. They're often highly driven and competitive, even in situations where it's not appropriate. Some of their intensity about achievement comes from trying to conquer their ADD symptoms. That's why some of our patients go can get downright obsessive—all as a way of trying to keep their lives together.

The Conscious Underachiever: Many with ADD shy away from challenges of any sort. They feel that it is better to venture nothing and gain nothing than to venture something and look stupid, foolish, or incompetent. They'll take jobs that are far too easy for them, ADD or not. They seek out what our adolescent patients label "dirtball" friends only because they're less likely to demand as much.

The conscious underachiever avoids anything that even smacks of potential failure. They subscribe to a sentiment expressed by the sportscaster Gary McCord: "Mediocrity knows no pressure."

The "Ditz": These folks tend to take the path of making a "virtue" out of a disability. They tend to define themselves as engagingly incompetent, spacey, and chronically needing others to assist them. This position of assumed incompetence serves to enlist the help of others. It says to people, "How can you expect an airhead like me to handle things maturely? If you were any kind of loving soul, you'd help poor me."

Actually, this isn't a bad strategy. It "excuses" you from certain responsibilities and seduces the aid of others. But the cost is that you come to be seen by others (and by yourself as well) as incompetent and somehow incapable of performing routine, day-to-day functions. It also fosters considerable dependency on the goodwill of your friends and family. They often tire of helping the ditz.

The Self-Medicator: Our clinical experience supports the notion that individuals with ADD are prone to substance abuse as a way of trying to self-treat their symptoms. Small amounts of alcohol can have a seemingly calming effect, and many individuals have in fact developed addictions or dependencies to control their symptoms.

You should know that the scientific evidence in the arena isn't as clear as the clinical lore (not an unusual circumstance). While some adults who have ADD may self-medicate, the higher rate of alcoholism could also be related to genetic factors, the emotional insults of having ADD, or simply the impulsive search for immediate gratification.

You can't help but adapt psychologically in response to an unusual strength or weakness. If you're exceptionally tall or talented at math or limited in your ability to express yourself with words, it's going to have an effect on how you adapt. And so, too, it is with extreme inattention and impulsiveness. These qualities will influence how you adjust to life's demands.

What strategies often work for ADD adults?

We're always cautious about offering lists of strategies as if each one will be successful for everyone. We have too much experience attending meetings of ADD adults and hearing contradictory experiences. Every time one person says, "You should really try this," someone pipes up, "Oh, I tried that and it didn't work for me."

Here's an example of how a standard suggestion for enhancing attention can help some yet hinder others: Open up most books on dealing with ADD and you'll be told to find a quiet place to work. "Remove all distractions," they'll tell you, "and you'll find it easier to concentrate." Makes sense and, for many, it's critical.

But it doesn't work that way for everyone. Many of our patients, young and old alike, fare poorly in distraction-free environments. It's too quiet for them to focus.

Some have found that they concentrate better with the TV on in the background or some quiet music playing. We have teenage clients who sincerely believe that their focus improves if they study with their head between two loudspeakers playing heavy metal music. They tell us it screens out all the other noises and forces them to focus. (Actually, there's some research to justify their claims.)

What helps our patients is to be familiar with a wide range of strategies and ideas. We make it clear that some might work while others might even make matters worse. If after a reasonable go of it one doesn't seem to fit your lifestyle or needs, move on to the next one. Just make sure you give it a reasonable shot. Short of medication, few things work immediately without some tinkering. And even getting the medication right requires experimentation.

We have another admission: Absolutely nothing we (or any of our colleagues) have to offer is other than common-sense compensations for inattention and impulsiveness. We don't want to give you the impression that we have well-researched techniques that are specifically designed for the ADD at heart. Our lists of suggestions, just like everyone else's, are sensible tips that our patients have found useful. They don't come out of systematic research or trials.

There's not one suggestion we've seen in any book or article on ADD that all God's creatures wouldn't be wise to follow. Who wouldn't be better off if he kept careful calendars, scheduled "blow off" time, systematically set priorities, and listened to feedback from others? What marriages wouldn't improve if partners communicated more openly and worked together to break down barriers to intimacy?

These kinds of recommendations benefit everyone, ADD or not. It's just that people with ADD must make a more concerted effort to incorporate them into daily life. What might be helpful tips to others are essential life supports for those who have ADD.

What's the Master Strategy for coping with ADD?

Before we started listing tips and strategies, we wanted to make sure we're clear about the general course of action you should pursue. This overall game plan holds for everyone with ADD. Actually it applies to all the planet's inhabitants. Herein lie the keys to adjustment:

The Two Commandments
for Coping with ADD,
Not to Mention Life Itself

~1~
Avoid situations
that are bound
to overwhelm you
with demands
you could never satisfy.

~2~
Once you find a
situation that's generally
manageable, tailor it to
maximize your strengths &
minimize your weaknesses.

We know we've just spouted the ultimate in common sense but, to quote Voltaire, "Common sense is not so common." And in the rush of daily life, it's not easy for anyone to step back and make decisions from a thoughtful distance. Often it takes a calamity of sorts to jar us into reflecting on our course.

For all of us, but especially for those with special needs, life is an unending series of compromises between dreams and realities. We've not met many people of any stripe who were able to accomplish all that they've imagined.

Some of us wanted to be famous musicians but couldn't carry a tune. Others dreamed about being doctors but had holes in our brains where calculus and chemistry problems are solved. To quote that esteemed philosopher and poet, Mick Jagger of the Rolling Stones, "You can't always get what you want, but if you try sometimes, you just might find you get what you need. Oh, yeah, baby, you get what you need."

What we're saying here is that you've got to learn which waves will swamp the boat. And even if those waves are in oceans you love, you'll need to stay clear of them. So if you're wildly distractible, don't pursue a career in air traffic control (please). If you're woefully impulsive and scattered, don't volunteer to organize the company picnic. If you have a terrible memory, the legal professions might not be for you.

We're not telling you to give up on pursuing your dreams. We just hope you pursue those that are attainable and not those that will only taunt you and cause you grief (see Principle 14). Life's hard enough as it is. You don't need to make it harder by setting yourself up for failure.

Once you settle into a situation you think you can handle, set upon a course of making it fit you. In the quest to adjust, we engineer our lives to minimize the hassles imposed by our limitations (and Lord knows we all have limitations).

If we're not good at details, we associate with detail-lovers or look to technology to lift the burdens. If we have a terrible sense of direction, we buy maps or have friends write down the exact route. If we're miserable proofreaders, we find eagle-eyed secretaries to comb through our reports and we make heavy use of spell-checkers.

Most of us benefit from regularly asking the question, "How can I avoid having to do too many things I'm likely to screw up?" Some may judge this as an exercise in finding the easy way out and as trashing the Rambo ethic. We prefer to see it as good problem solving.

Fine, but how about something more practical?

OK. Here's the list of suggestions our patients find most useful. Some are feasible, and others are pie in the sky, but worth knowing about. Whatever you do, don't limit your exploration to the tips on our list. All the books on Adult ADD have suggestions like these that are worth reviewing. Some of them might appeal to you:

► **Educate yourself.**

You can't solve a problem unless you understand it. By reading books, attending seminars, watching videos, talking to others, and participating in support groups, you can avoid the more obvious pitfalls. You'll benefit from the experiences of others and learn about a fuller range of options.

Reinventing well-worn wheels is a monumental waste of good time that could be better wasted on other activities. And in the arena of ADD, there are plenty of wheels and good ideas already on the road. There's just no substitute for becoming an expert on your own disorder.

► **Marry, room with, or otherwise befriend someone with fully functioning frontal lobes.**

Remember we told you that the frontal lobes of the brain are central to planning, self-control, and organization? Recall how most researchers consider them to be the missing brain link for individuals with ADD? Well, if you've got ADD, part of your life quest should be to associate with individuals with frontal lobes that operate at warp speed. All other things being equal, fall in love with a pair of frontal lobes.

We're not suggesting you search for people to care for you or on whom you should become overly dependent. Relationships designed only to correct defects or fulfill needs are almost always doomed. But if that man with the cute

---

smile or that woman with the mesmerizing eyes also happens to be into organization and reasonable tolerance, all the better.

Now if you're ADD and already attached, odds are you've connected with a partner whose frontal lobes are fully functional. At least that's how balances and complementarities in relationships tend to work. Don't feel bad. You might leave dishes around and forget appointments, but your energy and spontaneity probably make for some good times. If not, you're no doubt giving a would be Mother Theresa or Father Flanagan a worthy cause.

So, if you're single, next time you walk into a bar, don't ask, "Are you a Pisces?" or "Don't I know you?" March right up and say, "Pardon me, but are your frontal lobes working?" If you've already hooked up with a good pair of frontal lobes, put this book down, walk over to your partner, and let loose with a heartfelt hug and kiss.

Associating with attentive and organized people is the single most powerful coping strategy we can offer. Luckily, for every person in this world who concentrates too little on details there's at least one other who worries too much about them. Locate these people, marry them, hire them, be good to them, and keep them near.

► **Keep it simple.**

The K.I.S.S. (Keep It Simple Stupid) rule of problem solving has much to offer the ADD adult. The more complicated a strategy, the more likely you'll have problems incorporating it over the long haul. That's why so many of our patients have trouble with the fancy organizational techniques offered by experts unfamiliar with ADD. The more you can pare down routines to their most basic elements, the more you'll repeat them.

If you work with parents and teachers of ADD children, you develop a special appreciation for the benefits of simplicity. Our storage areas are filled with comprehensive management programs that, while conceptually sound, are too impractical and time-consuming. What works best is what's simple enough to use day after day. If it sounds too complicated to you, it probably won't work for long.

► **Do it now!**

This advice is a consistent element of all the books and programs we've seen on personal organization. It's also a strategy we hear about routinely from our best-adjusted patients. What does it mean? If someone hands you a phone message, don't put the slip down on your desk. Call back immediately. If you're delivered a report to review, don't set it on a pile. Read it right away. Did your wife just ask you to call the restaurant for reservations? Don't wait. Do it now. Every moment that passes notches up the chances that a task won't get completed.

A related strategy that works for some of us is what we'll call "Worst First." If you have three pressing matters before you, start with the most onerous one. Get it out of the way so that you can move on to the next one. Knowing you've dealt with the worst motivates you to tackle the rest.

▶ **Make every door your signal to STOP and THINK.**

If you're at all impulsive, you'll benefit from any trick that will get you to stop and think before dashing off. Some of our patients have their computers or organizers beep every half hour to remind them to check their "To Do" list. Others request that partners and coworkers stop them before leaving home or the office and ask, "Do you have everything you need?"

A common technique is to use doors as cues to stop and think. As one of our patients told us, "The best thing I ever did was to train myself to treat doors like traffic lights. Every time I start to walk through one I stop myself to ask, 'What do I need? What did I forget to do or to take?'" Since doors are everywhere, they're architectural versions of reminder strings tied around your finger.

▶ **Have duplicates of everything that's important.**

Especially your keys. Triplicates, even. Keep a set in your car, in your home, in your briefcase or backpack, and on your person.

For their ADD youngsters, parents and

---

teachers learn that duplicates of essential items are a must. Often children have two sets of texts (one for home and another for school). They also have extra sneakers, gloves, and coats stashed here, there, and everywhere.

▶ **Write it down!**

We know that it's an incredible pain, but there is just no substitute for writing things down. What's on paper is easier to retrieve than memos in the mind. If it's important, write it down.

But don't just write it on napkins or gas receipts. Have a notepad surgically implanted on your forearm and a pen fused to your index finger if that's what it takes to have a memo system at your immediate disposal.

One of our college students wears a pen around his neck and writes memos on his hand. He figures that he has a better chance of holding on to his appendages than to a piece of paper. We like that kind of attitude in a patient.

The trick is to write down memos and thoughts the instant they come into your head. Wait even a minute and you could lose them forever.

▶ **Make "Post-its" your friend.**

While we don't advocate Post-its for making lists or for ongoing note making, they are great for making yourself reminders. They work best when affixed to computer screens, steering wheels, wallets, and anything else you have trouble overlooking. You'll have to train yourself to use them, but they might just help.

▶ **Try out time management strategies.**

If you have ADD, time is your constant enemy. You never have enough of it, you don't use it efficiently when you've got it, and you rarely have a sense of its passing. The ADD anthem could well be Judy Collins' song, "Who Knows Where the Time Goes?"

Common sense tells us that, if someone has problems managing time, we should simply teach him time management skills. And, indeed, there are lists and lists of suggestions in ADD guides and non-ADD publications. On a recent visit to a bookstore, we found about a dozen titles dedicated to personal organization and time management. At the office supply emporium next door were several shelves of organizers and time management aids.

Here's the problem: Most of our patients ultimately derive little help from these books or programs. The trouble seems to be that they often require a great deal of organizational ability and discipline to follow. You must remember to write everything down in certain sections or reflect enough to prioritize your activities systematically. The bad organizational habits of individuals with ADD are so deeply ingrained and so central to the disorder that complicated programs won't help much.

We've heard an oft-repeated complaint about these programs: They require so much discipline that, if you can use them, you're probably not seriously ADD. Time management programs assume more frustration tolerance and inhibition than most with ADD can manage.

Also, time management tasks aren't famous for being interesting or stimulating. Some of the books we've seen are filled with charts, priority lists, and complicated calendars. While they might work for non-ADD sorts, they're usually way beyond the organizational capacity of our patients.

Wanna make a million? Design an organizational program that most ADD adults will truly find useful for more than a week. The kit should likely contain the following:

- A list of powerful incentives for getting work completed. These might include coupons for food, drink, sensual pleasures, promotions, and free time for sporting activities.
- A list of powerful sanctions for not getting things done. These might include dismissal notices, divorce decrees, and restrictions from sensual pleasures and sporting activities.
- An auxiliary pair of frontal lobes to negotiate and administer a program of rewards and punishments.
- A work enrichment technician who makes

sure that all tasks are as motivating, compelling, and enjoyable as possible to you personally.

- A "chunking" engineer who will break tasks into digestible chunks that you can complete without going nuts.
- A self-esteem cheerleader who will keep your spirits up when work demands are overwhelming.

Because we haven't found such a program yet, perhaps you should take a look at what's available now. If you find an approach that seems reasonable, by all means try it. Just don't be discouraged if it turns out to be too complicated. Even if the grand program is overly detailed, you might nonetheless discover a strategy or two that are worthwhile.

▶ **Make use of technology.**

These days there are dozens of electronic gadgets that might simplify your life. You can usually find them in Sharper Image catalogs or at the office supply store. For example, many of us have developed intimate relationships with our electronic organizers and schedulers. We keep them near our hearts at all times. They are the repository for every idea, reminder, and deadline that happens upon us during the day.

New on the scene are what amount to digitized voice recorders. They're the size of credit cards and record a minute or two of reminders and ideas. Our patients seem to like them because they don't entail writing anything down. They keep them in their shirt pockets or around their necks on a chain.

But the all-time, number one gadget that's most helped our patients is the personal computer. With its spell- and grammar-checkers, alarm functions, database managers, planning tools, E-mail, and faxes, a PC is a gold mine of aid to the seriously disorganized. It's a hell of a lot easier to find a document that's on a computer than one that's buried in clutter. Computers are to ADD adults what crutches are to the lame.

Coping with ADD is a lifelong crusade. What works one day might fall by the wayside the next. Sometimes effective strategies lose their impact only because they're no longer new and interesting. But be assured that small successes in organization pile up to make for some big changes. A little cleverness goes a long way.

If you could rule the world, what changes would you make to help people with ADD?

It's always fun to devise wish lists. Hey, you never know when you'll win the lottery or be asked by a grateful nation to redesign society as we know it. Because we didn't think it would be fair to keep our preliminary list private, here it is:

▶ Form a version of AA for adults with ADD. Group support is remarkable. It beats some guy with a beard lecturing you or deftly attempting to stimulate your emotions.

► Establish "Centers for Vocational Decision Making and Training" in every neighborhood. They would be available to all citizens who needed help identifying their strengths and weaknesses, making decisions about careers, and adjusting to occupational demands. They would also house down-to-earth efficiency/organizational counselors.

► Require true career counseling for every student.

► Limit the number of times per year talk shows can air sensationalized programs about ADD.

► Arrange for all paychecks to be electronically deposited.

► Establish automatic deduction of utilities, rent, and mortgage payments from paychecks.

► Equip all keys and TV remotes with location finders.

► Require all spouses, partners, offspring, friends, and coworkers to become super-organized and appropriately tolerant.

► Make all bosses minimize requirements for paper shuffling and record keeping.

► Automate payments for travel, food, and lodging so that all receipts are automatically recorded, organized, and submitted for reimbursement and tax filings.

► Lower classification for stimulants so that they could be more easily prescribed.

► Force absolutely all human service providers

(from physicians to teachers to mental health professionals) to take a course on the identification and treatment of ADD.

Why haven't you offered more ways I can improve my relationships with others?

We just don't know what to say that hasn't already been covered in shelf after shelf of self-help books. Because research regarding the impact of Adult ADD on relationships hasn't been conducted, we can't provide advice that's unique or especially tailored.

We can only state the obvious: living with someone who has ADD has its challenges. And they go beyond just having to deal with someone who's disorganized and unreliable. We're also talking about the struggles that arise from maintaining emotional closeness with a partner who is often inattentive, impulsive, frustrated, and moody.

Couples who cope with the ADD factor are wise to talk openly about its impact on their relationship. They often have to make a special effort to communicate honestly and to solve problems cooperatively. And if reading all those self-help books isn't enough to grease the wheels of a squeaky relationship, you should read the next section carefully.

That all having been said, we don't want to leave you without offering at least a few tips for improving your success in loving relationships. So, with our tongues firmly parked in our cheeks, here it is:

The Gordon and McClure Guide to Improving Your Relationships with the Opposite Sex

If you're a man, never say:	If you're a woman, never say:
► Your hormones must be acting up again.	► I'm almost positive you're the baby's father.
► You know I would've shown up for our anniversary if I didn't have to go hunting.	► You still needed those old baseball cards?
► That's definitely a woman's job.	► How many side view mirrors did that car come with originally?
► Maybe you are putting on a pound or two.	► What I wouldn't do for a night alone with Fabio.
► Hey, I was drunk. How was I supposed to know she was your sister?	► You've got to admire Lorena Bobbitt's assertiveness.
► Who gives a damn if I left the toilet seat up?	► Why can't we just cuddle?
	► Who would've thought you'd go bald so quickly?

Do you think if the ADD business goes sour either of us has a future as the next Leo Buscalia or Thomas Moore? Probably not. But maybe Hallmark will call us to write lines for those "walk on the beach in the warm sunset" cards that communicate sentiments of love and romance.

Beyond all these practical strategies for coping with ADD, is there a role for psychotherapy?

Psychotherapy has generally gotten a bad rap in ADD circles. For helping children, pills, parenting, and practical educational techniques usually take precedence over puppets and play therapy.

Some of us have gotten frustrated with clinicians who deal with ADD as if it were related to inner conflicts. There's too much evidence that it's more of a neurobiological phenomenon. No amount of playing checkers or the board game *Sorry* will dissolve the impact of ADD.

While psychotherapy might not improve the core symptoms of the disorder, it can nonetheless play a role within a treatment program (even for young children). First off, psychotherapy might address those conditions that often coexist with ADD, such as depression, the reaction to trauma, or family distress. Ongoing counseling can also help with the inevitable self-esteem issues and with keeping patients motivated and on track. As we've mentioned often, having ADD over a lifetime creates a planeload of excess emotional baggage, much of which won't disappear with a dose of medication. Therapy, marital and otherwise, can play a role in improving the lot of those who live with ADD.

Of all the reasons you might want to establish an ongoing relationship with a therapist, these are the most common and compelling:

- ► You want someone who can serve as an information source about a wide range of issues that might arise.
- ► You need an authoritative advocate in dealing with schools, employers, and family.
- ► You're having trouble coping with frustration, insecurity, and anxiety.
- ► You can't get beyond the remorse, anger, and upset that was generated by the diagnosis.
- ► Even though you've read dozens of self-help books, you can't quite make the advice fit your needs.
- ► You don't make changes well unless someone is right there to offer encouragement, support, advice, and hope.
- ► Your partner has begged, pleaded with, and threatened you to resolve certain personal, marital, or family issues.

Most of us who treat ADD patients find ourselves routinely stretching the boundaries of the therapist's traditional role. We offer services and perform functions that our training supervisors would have surely frowned upon. Who would have thought we'd be providing what amounts to career guidance, job counseling, straightforward encouragement, and education regarding pharmacotherapy?

In discussions with colleagues who work with an ADD clientele, we've had confirmation of our own experience: To be helpful, we've got to be comfortable wearing a closetful of different hats. We've listed here a sampling of the roles we might play:

- Educator
- Advocate
- Negotiator (between our patients and their schools or work)
- Cheerleader/Motivator
- Career counselor
- Grief counselor
- Family therapist
- Individual therapist
- Marital counselor
- Group therapist
- Consultant to support organizations, schools, and employers
- Organizational expert
- Legal advisor (as opposed to lawyer)

Which flavor of mental health provider makes for the best therapist?

We have the same answer we offered when we discussed who makes the best diagnostician: whoever is most informed, flexible, cooperative, and approachable. No set of degrees insures any of those qualities.

Just make certain that whoever you're working with has more than a passing knowledge about ADD. You'll want a therapist who can make decisions about treatment based upon a thorough understanding of your disorder. This also goes for any organizational consultants or efficiency experts you might hire. (We refer you back to Principle 6, pages 76 to 79, for a discussion of traits that are desirable in clinicians.)

Having pronounced the importance of picking an ADD-competent therapist, we must bow again to the winds of reality: Not many therapists or consultants are truly knowledgeable about ADD. The professional community is generally camped at the beginning stretches of the learning curve.

An attendee at one of our workshops suggested that we publish a pop quiz about ADD that you could administer to prospective therapists. Could you imagine? You'd sit down at your first appointment and announce to the therapist, "Before we proceed, I wonder if you might take out a clean sheet of paper, a number two pencil, and write your name in the top right-hand corner. I will ask you 10 True/False questions about ADD. If you answer at least 8 correctly, I'll tell you about my psychological problems."

Maybe the quiz would look something like this:

1. True/False   Individuals who have ADD are born with biological vulnerabilities toward inattention and poor self-control. (true)

2. True/False   ADD children usually outgrow their symptoms by adolescence. (false)

3. True/False   ADD adults would do just fine if they only tried harder to be responsible. (false)

4. True/False   ADD is caused by poor parenting, sugar, or food additives. (false)

5. True/False   ADD can be inherited. (true)

6. True/False   All ADD individuals concentrate best in quiet, sterile environments. (false)

7. True/False   Antidepressants are as safe and effective as stimulants for most adults who have ADD. (false)

8. True/False   Stimulant medications often cause serious side effects, such as changes in personality and growth retardation. (false)

9. True/False   Women can suffer from ADD. (true)

10. True/False   Counseling is almost always unnecessary for those ADD patients who respond to medication. (false)

Hey, we might have just revolutionized the entire health care system. Our little 10-item pop quiz could be the beginning of a new movement: "Patient-Administered Practitioner Competence Testing." You need an acronym for these programs, so we'll use PAPCOMTEST. We'd better wait by the phone for inquiries about our approach from Congress, health care planners, and insurance industry executives. We're sure they'll call by the dozens.

Principle **12**

You can't pick your relatives, but you can pick your college.

If most of our ADD patients had the option, they'd avoid educational institutions like the proverbial plague. Why would anyone who has trouble sitting and concentrating willingly subject themselves to endless hours of demands for sitting and concentration? For individuals with ADD, schools are simply cosmic walls against which heads are banged every day.

But unless you're independently wealthy, a kept man or woman, or maybe a drug dealer, school is important for success. Nowadays there just aren't too many vocational options that don't require advanced training beyond high school.

Our advice about college follows closely the Master Game Plan we discussed on page 149. To remind you of those commandments, here they are again:

> ## The Two Commandments for Coping with ADD, Not to Mention Life Itself
>
> **~1~**
> Avoid situations that are bound to overwhelm you with demands you could never satisfy.
>
> **~2~**
> Once you find a situation that's generally manageable, tailor it to maximize your strengths & minimize your weaknesses.

For college-related decisions, these commandments must be followed with special caution if you're going to avoid more than the normal heartache. They can be applied to educational environments by what we call the "Three Rules for Surviving Higher Education."

▶ Decide if college is really for you.

▶ If you opt to attend college, choose wisely.

▶ When you get to college, miss no opportunity to tailor it to your needs.

We'll take each rule in turn:

To matriculate or not to matriculate, that is the question

We have no special magic for deciding whether it's wise for you to attend college. We just advise that you give it serious thought before automatically moving along the road to higher education. If it's pretty certain that collegiate demands will overwhelm you, give some serious consideration to your alternatives.

We've noticed that many of our patients in high school harbor the fantasy that getting away from home will solve all their ills. "My life will be fine," we hear, "if I can just get away from my parents' nagging and their over-involvement in my life."

But then these students travel off to college and discover that they needed some of that nagging and overinvolvement to accomplish anything. Without parents and teachers looking over their shoulders, many of our ADD students lose their way.

Our patients also discover that, while college allows for more freedom, demands for attention and organization skyrocket. You have less supervision and support in the classroom as well as with more long-term projects. You also have to manage the details of everyday life (like laundry and shopping).

Now we're aware that there are ways of making college manageable. We also know that, in some respects, students can fare better in college because they're often better able to tailor course work to meet their interests and talents. College is unquestionably an option for many of our patients, but not for all of them.

For those who don't go to a four-year college, opportunities are plentiful. Some have done well in technical trade schools that teach electronics, computer sciences, and other skills. The advantage of these schools is that they focus more quickly on an individual's strengths and interests. If you're good at mechanics and enjoy working with machines, it's exciting to get right to it and learn the trade. For many, it beats having to wade through core curriculum courses on human civilization and art history.

Others we've worked with have gone right to a job, often in marketing. They realize their strengths lie in their enthusiasm and people skills, so they find positions that call for those qualities. We've noticed that several have stopped by our offices to say hello in cars dramatically nicer than our own. And still other patients pursue experiences in drama, art, and music. (One young fellow we know plays blues guitar with such death-defying skill that he went right on to a career in the entertainment industry.)

If you do go to college, find one that's ADD-friendly

If you attend a college with class sizes that are huge and professors who are marginally involved with individual students, you'll be in trouble for sure. Ivy on the walls won't help you survive lectures with a hundred students in them, particularly if you had trouble with high school classes of 30.

Your goal in selecting a college is to find one that bears an uncanny resemblance to a high school-resource room. You have to look for environments that have the following attributes:

- ▶ Small class sizes
- ▶ Rampant opportunities for individualized attention
- ▶ High levels of structure and supervision
- ▶ Professors who make learning exciting and fun

▶ A sincere willingness to make reasonable accommodations

▶ An understanding of ADD

At the end of this book you'll find a listing of college guides for students with special needs. You can also get names from CH.A.D.D. and other support organizations. Perhaps your best sources of information are friends or acquaintances who have already been through the process.

When you interview at a college, you'll want to ask about:

▶ Class size

▶ Availability and variety of academic support services

▶ Whether counselors and administrators are familiar with ADD

▶ Access to computer services

▶ Physical layout (Are essential buildings easy to find or are they spread out over a large area?)

▶ How easy it is to re-enter if you needed to take a semester or two off during the course of your education

▶ The sophistication of physicians in the student health service about ADD and ADD-related medications

▶ Whether counseling and support groups are available

It's an especially good idea to talk to some of the juniors and seniors about their experiences. Ask them about the quality of the faculty, about opportunities for extra help, and about the college's overall level of dedication to helping all students.

Attending college is an expensive, time-consuming proposition. The hours and energy you spend trying to find a setting that fits your style will reap dividends for you in the future. For many of our patients, that process has led them to enroll in smaller colleges with a special interest in working with students requiring more intensive support.

Before you unpack your trunk, head for the academic support center

We admire anyone who wants to handle college life with as little assistance as possible. The collegiate years aren't exactly times when you relish making contact with people who look over your shoulder or question your judgment.

But the chances are sky-high that you'll need some form of extra help adjusting to college life. If you don't require that assistance, you've either discovered ADD University or you're not as bad off as you thought.

Nearly all colleges and universities now have centers for helping students with special needs. While they go by various titles (we've heard names like Academic Support Services, Office of Special Services, and Learning Disabilities Program), they all are designed to help students meet academic demands.

You'll likely find a variety of service providers, from tutors to note takers to advocates to counselors. They might also help you acquire reasonable accommodations, perhaps of the sort you enjoyed in your secondary education. These might include extra time taking tests or special check-in times with professors to make sure you're on track with long-term assignments.

Be aware that, if you've been labeled or diagnosed as having ADD, you're entitled to those services by law (see *ADD and the College Student,* listed in the Resources section). If you've chosen your college carefully and the people in admissions were honest with you, you shouldn't need to work hard at getting services. But you never know.

Principle **13**

Don't play third base if you can't throw.

We want to keep hammering at a central theme of our advice for ADD compensations: Before you worry about which organizer to buy or how to approach your boss, make sure you're in a job that highlights your gifts and not your inadequacies.

Given the ever-increasing technological nature of our society, it's hard to avoid jobs that require concentration. But you can at least minimize or work around those demands. Unfortunately, some of us are so driven to overcome our most serious faults that we dive into occupations that are bound to overwhelm us. And once in a no-win situation, we become frustrated with ourselves and perhaps also with the system.

We're encouraged that our young adult patients are more often asking us the question, "What kind of career do you think someone with ADD should pursue?" By posing that question, they're showing evidence of making decisions based on what's sensible and not just on what's lucrative or intriguing.

Now having praised them for asking us the question, we have to tell you that we're not apt to offer specific

---

recommendations. So much depends on an individual's personality and array of talents.

The most obvious characteristics of a suitable career are listed here. They're variants of common sense and those Two Commandments we keep talking about:

Five Rules for Choosing a Job
If You Have ADD
(and even if you don't):

▶ Choose a job that capitalizes on your talents ("If you can't throw, don't . . .").

▶ Only insert yourself in work situations you have a snowball's chance of managing. (Because one of our patients was highly skilled at math, she chose to pursue a career in tax accounting. For her, a bad idea.)

▶ Choose a job that you find fascinating.

▶ Only work in places that allow for some compensation and accommodation.

▶ Never stop thinking up ways of reducing demands for organization.

Unfortunately, you don't really know how a career works until you've tried it. Even within a career path there can be jobs that vary widely in ADD-suitability.

What specific job settings should I look for?

We always figure that, if you have to go to work, it might as well be fun and manageable. Sure, work can be rewarding and fulfilling. Be honest, though. Would you rather be toiling at a computer or lazily fishing for bass in a secluded pond, playing tennis, or just sitting home and staring idiotically at the TV?

Especially if you have ADD, fun work is the work that you'll most often complete on time. You'll be more likely to attend to whatever is most compelling at the moment. The more your work has that quality, the better.

We went through our records and listed the jobs our better-adjusted ADD adults have settled into. Don't take our list too seriously, though, because it reflects the nature of our clientele (those who get referred to us) and the availability of jobs in our areas. But we've both been intrigued by the commonalities. You'll notice that the most popular are those that require little long-term planning, have an intensity about them, and involve people.

- ► EMT technicians—A very popular choice among our patients because it's high on excitement and low on long-term planning. Coworkers are often stunned by how focused a usually disorganized soul can be when there's urgency and ample adrenaline flowing.
- ► Real estate agents—They have plenty of opportunity to move about, work with people, and get caught up in the thrill of the hunt for prospects. Also, lawyers and banks oversee the critical details.
- ► Marketing/Sales (especially if it involves travel and personal contact).

- Pizza delivery (for teenagers)—Maybe we're seeing a select group, but we've not been surprised by the problems national chains are having with the accident rates of their drivers.

- Professors of child psychology who specialize in ADD—We're mostly kidding here. But academic life isn't necessarily a bad place if you have ADD. Most professors have days that are largely unstructured, save for a fixed schedule of classes. The day affords opportunities for diversity (teach a class, work in the lab, meet with some students, go to a meeting).

  Academic life, whether you're a child psychologist or not, often allows you to sharply narrow your focus to just what interests you. One of our patients is internationally known for his expertise in the mating habits of certain insects. For reasons only his analyst knows for sure, this fellow is absolutely fascinated by how these bugs procreate. He spends little time in an office and has graduate students tend to the tedious work of literature searches and initial drafts.

- Military personnel—Military life is a highly structured existence. In fact, by its nature it contains many of the essential elements of an ideal environment for someone who has ADD. Think about it: The rules are extremely clear and regimented, the consequences for compliance are meaningful and compelling, and many of the assigned tasks are intense (like getting shot at) and involve physical activity. As you read earlier in John's case, not everyone handles the rules well. But many cling to the structure and function at their best when routines are so clearly set and enforced. We wish we had a dollar for every patient who told us, "You know, I did just fine in the military. When I was discharged, though, everything fell apart."

▶ Forest and park rangers—Although many such positions are low on moment-to-moment excitement, they're also low on office work requirements. One of our patients held a higher degree in engineering and spent 10 years struggling to hold an office job. It became so dispiriting that he got to the point where suicide seemed like an attractive option. Instead, he left his job in an engineering firm to become an inspector for a park system. He now spends most of his day driving or walking about to ensure that certain equipment runs properly. He told us that he's never been happier.

To be a bit more specific, here's a list of questions you should ask yourself as you consider various employment options:

▶ Are the job demands generally manageable?
▶ Does it hold the potential to generate the income you need to live in a lifestyle that's comfortable for you?
▶ Are there good benefits, especially for medical insurance?

- ▶ Are resources available that you can draw upon for help in accommodating? Efficient secretaries, employee assistance counselors, and modern computing systems can be invaluable.

- ▶ Will coworkers/bosses be reasonably sympathetic? There's no better compensation than working with decent people who are supportive and willing to solve problems productively.

Should someone with a chronic impulse control disorder become a gun-carrying police officer?

We posed this question with the sole intent of being provocative. It's one that individuals as well as society at large struggle to address. And it's complicated.

With passage of the Americans with Disabilities Act and the Rehabilitation Act of 1973, in addition to actions by agencies involved in ensuring equal opportunities, individuals with ADD have legal rights in the workplace. These are carefully described in a book by the Lathams, *Succeeding in the Workplace* (see Resources section). These laws and regulations all stipulate reasonable accommodations and certain job protections.

In essence, these various rules represent the adult version of the special education laws that mandate services for children with special needs. They also prevent employers from not hiring you or from firing you simply because you have ADD.

You should unquestionably know your rights and use legal recourse where appropriate. But if you haven't already, we want to get you thinking about times when having rights and doing what's right might collide.

Here's another real-life scenario that illustrates the quandaries that employees, employers, and clinicians can find themselves grappling with:

Thank the Lord I missed

Ben was a police officer in a small town. For several years he had no problems carrying out his responsibilities on the beat. Job performance reviews, however, were highly critical of his disorganization and failure to complete paperwork. Although his colleagues covered for him as best they could, his sloppiness affected the outcome of several prosecutions.

Aside from his messiness and despite a long history of impulsive behavior, Ben refrained from any serious poor judgment on the job. Fortunately, his beat was almost always quiet. He rarely found himself in highly charged situations.

Ben's personal life was tumultuous because he let loose with his temper far too often. He also drank off the job more than was wise. Unfortunately, he avoided seeking help for his drinking out of fear he'd lose his job.

Because his persistent disorganization was such an issue at work, Ben made an appointment for an ADD evaluation, completed all the forms, and arrived for an initial interview. All signs pointed to ADD as the diagnosis. But Ben didn't show for any further appointments because he again was afraid that a diagnosis would interfere with his career.

One afternoon the dispatcher told him that a robbery suspect was seen heading for a park in Ben's district. Ben drove to that location, got out of the car, and saw a young man entering the park. Without thinking and somewhat charged up by the excitement, Ben drew his gun and ran toward the suspect. The fellow turned abruptly and drew what Ben thought was a gun. Ben discharged his revolver and blessedly missed.

The terrified subject threw up his arms and identified himself as a college student who was walking through the park. His "gun" was just a tape player.

Ben was severely reprimanded for this incident. Several months later, he was again disciplined for poor restraint in the handling of a domestic dispute.

Because these events were obviously troublesome to Ben, he wanted to get help. After consulting a lawyer he learned that, while he couldn't be fired for being identified as ADD, he could be dismissed for taking Ritalin. After much soul-searching, Ben chose to resign from law enforcement.

These cases raise thorny issues for all of us: Should someone with ADD be allowed to carry a weapon? Work as a pilot or air traffic controller? Does it make sense that getting help for a problem should be grounds for dismissal in certain professions? Should you tell a prospective employer about your problems at the interview? Just because someone has the right to work, should he exercise it if it means putting others at risk? What are the clinician's responsibilities?

As always, the answers to these questions depend on individual circumstance. And these dilemmas are surely not limited to ADD. They also hold for drug addictions, depression, and most other serious problems. But they're important to think about, especially in considering whether you're suitable for particular jobs.

What are some strategies for long-term job success?

▶ Don't let yourself get promoted to your level of incompetence.

▶ Surround yourself with those frontal lobes.

▶ Never stop delegating.

▶ Never stop looking for ways to ease the burden.

Remember the Peter Principle of the 1970s? It held that individuals rise in an organization until they reach a position that they can no longer handle competently. We see this happening quickly to many of our ADD patients. After mastering a job that suits their style and talents, they're promoted to positions that fit them poorly. And the consequences can be serious. Here is another example:

"Please Demote Me, Let Me Go"

Arlene was diagnosed with ADD in grade school because of a wildly impulsive style. While she responded well to medication and worked hard to compensate, she still qualified for that diagnosis as an adult.

After several years of unsuccessful employment, Arlene landed a job as a marketing representative for a small pharmaceutical company (no, they don't make stimulants). She flourished in this position because it involved lots of activity and only a little organization.

With her vibrant personality and people skills, Arlene had no trouble making a name for herself as a top salesperson. It didn't hurt that her coworker enjoyed handling traveling arrangements, scheduling hospital contacts, and managing other details of the job.

After about four years in this position, Arlene was promoted to management. Her responsibilities now included tracking sales, keeping tabs on a sizeable sales force, and preparing reports for upper management.

Absolutely inundated by demands for organization, Arlene began to sink both on the job and in her personal life. She told her counselor, "There's not enough Ritalin in the world to help me do this job." She became so stressed that she actually was hospitalized for chest pains.

Following several sessions talking with her counselor, Arlene returned to her supervisor and requested a demotion to the sales force. Her boss, by that point well aware of how much she had struggled, agreed. While

Arlene was disappointed by her inability to handle the promotion, she told us she doesn't regret her decision for a second.

Could you get more specific about how to adjust at work?

The best way we could think of to communicate the spirit of this enterprise is to tell you about a friend of ours who was recently diagnosed with ADD. He nonetheless has been compensating his whole life.

Driving (a Golf Ball) to Distraction

Bobby is a long hitter and head golf pro at an exclusive club in the South. Born on a farm in a small Mississippi town, he always underachieved. Yet he was able to just make it through college with gentleman Cs. A talented golfer and teacher, he decided to capitalize on his gifts and became an assistant pro at a small club.

Bobby functioned especially well in this position. He spent much of his time giving brief lessons, romping around the course, or focusing on time-limited projects. Although he worked harder than the others to accomplish the same tasks, he adjusted fairly well. After awhile, though, he was finding himself increasingly fatigued and depressed, especially at the end of the season.

As time passed, Bobby's aspirations and responsibilities grew. Now in his 40s, he took a coveted job as head golf pro at this renowned country club. In his position as head pro he's expected to manage a staff of 20, order inventory and track sales at the pro shop, organize a full schedule of events, and maintain the expected air of affability and good cheer.

It just about killed him. He was treated for depression and also was at some peril of losing his job. The diagnosis of ADD and some medication have turned his life around from a bogey to at least a par.

Medication or not, Bobby has compensated for his inattentive style in many ways. On a visit, we asked him to make a list of the kinds of things he's done to make life easier at work. Many of those adjustments hinge on his careful selection and deployment of staff. (At home, he compensated in large part by marrying a compassionate and delightful pair of frontal lobes).

Here is Bobby's list:

▶ Changed his office from near the main reception desk to an abandoned caddy shack. (It's not unusual to receive 200 calls a day in a pro shop.)
▶ Put a phone in his private office that allows only outgoing calls.
▶ Delegated all detail work to detail-oriented assistant pro.
▶ Computerized sales. (He actually delegated that project.)
▶ Told staff about his ADD.
▶ Told management about his ADD.

Principle 13

- ▶ Schedules teaching appointments for 45 minutes even though he could make more money if there were 30 minutes long. He uses the extra fifteen minutes as a cushion.

- ▶ Never schedules an appointment himself. Sends all students to main desk for scheduling.

- ▶ Staff prepares an index card for him that contains a listing of all the day's appointments.

- ▶ Comes in an hour earlier than the rest of the staff so he can have an uninterrupted block of time to get organized.

- ▶ Lives close to the course so that he has more time to finish his work.

- ▶ Bought a computer for word processing.

Should I tell job interviewers I've got ADD?

We constantly struggle with this question, as do our colleagues and patients. And, after years of consideration, this is what we can tell you with absolute certainty: There's no stock answer. It really does depend on individual circumstance.

In the best of all worlds, you would be open and honest from the outset about whatever limitations you might have. You would tell interviewers about anything that might get in the way of fulfilling your job responsibilities. Armed with full disclosure (and impressed by your candor), a potential employer could make an informed hiring decision. If he decided to hire you, he would arrange for whatever accommodations might be necessary and work with you along the way to optimize your performance.

That's in the best of all worlds, the exact location of which we're not entirely sure (we've heard it might be somewhere in South Carolina). In other locales, such progressive personnel management hasn't uniformly taken hold. Chances are an employer would be far less inclined to hire you if he knew you were chronically and seriously disorganized and impulsive. If you had such a history but were successfully treated with medication, that might be a different story. But a diagnosis of ADD isn't generally regarded as a plus on your resume.

How about once I'm hired?

A somewhat less tricky question. But the answer again resides in your judgment of the players involved and of the potential benefits and risks of such disclosure. Typically, these are the issues to consider:

- ▶ Are my supervisors decent and mature enough to handle my disclosure productively?
- ▶ Are my coworkers decent and mature enough to handle my disclosure productively?
- ▶ What might disclosure accomplish for me on the job? Help with compensating? A little more time to get things done? Some understanding?
- ▶ How might talking about my ADD make matters worse on the job? Will people have trouble seeing me as competent? Will it be held against me in assignments or promotions?

If you do decide to discuss ADD at work, you might want to keep in mind the following ideas:

▶ Don't wait until you're about to get fired or you're in the middle of a major problem to tell the boss. If it looks like you're approaching doom, you'd better let him know what might be getting in your way. At least you can give him and you a chance to problem solve together. The best disasters are those anticipated and avoided.

▶ Be prepared to educate colleagues in the workplace. They don't need to know all the details, but certain elements are critical:

- It's not a cheap excuse but a legitimate disorder.

- You've had a competent evaluation so it's not that you're looking to avoid responsibility by fabricating a disorder.

- You realize you still have responsibility for your actions, ADD or not. You're just hoping people might understand why you might have trouble with certain tasks.

- If anyone wants to know how he might help, you'd like to talk to him about it. He should understand that most of the assistance you'd be looking for is in minimizing, however possible, demands for organization and detail management.

▶ Don't wear your ADD like a badge of honor and go around as if people owe you something because you've got a problem. The legal rights you're entitled to by dint of

---

Principle 13 191

your disorder don't free you to carry forth with a sense of entitlement.

▶ Having ADD isn't exactly like admitting you're a serial killer or child molester. While your colleagues might not be familiar with the specifics, enough information has filtered through the popular press to raise public awareness. Many of our patients have obsessed for months about whether to disclose their diagnosis only to be surprised by a matter-of-fact, supportive response.

If we've learned anything about life, it's that events more often hinge not on what you do but how you do it. If you strut in to see a boss with a chip on your shoulder, inform him of your rights, and make it clear what you expect, you'll be asking for trouble. But providing him information as a way of respectfully enlisting his input and support might just work.

Any final words of wisdom about coping with ADD?

When we work with ADD families, we always try to promote a problem-solving spirit. While our patients often look first for quick salvation or someone else to blame, eventually they settle down to seeing their ADD as a challenge that can be managed. Coping with problems in any realm of life involves following these steps:

1. Identifying the problem or goal
2. Formulating alternatives
3. Trying out those alternatives
4. Using feedback to pick, choose, and modify strategies
5. Engineering situations so those solutions get implemented

Our most successful patients don't see their ADD as a handicap or an excuse or a cross to bear or a claim to fame. They regard it as a problem that can be controlled with some cleverness, support, patience, and good fortune.

Principle **14**

Keep your eyes on the prize.

We want to end our book by offering one last caution: Don't get so caught up in overcoming your ADD that you forget to enjoy life. While improving productivity and performance are noble goals, we all have limits to how much we can maximize our talents and desires. None of us, ADD or not, benefit ultimately from a preoccupation with perfection.

Why in the world are we sounding such a laid-back, "Do the best you can" theme? Are we telling you to curb your aspirations and settle for less? Just because you have a limitation, does that mean you shouldn't strive for the best?

Of course not. We've written an entire book filled with suggestions for making positive changes. Having ADD isn't a prescription for misery or failure. It's a problem that can be managed.

For our ADD patients who aren't careful, life can become an all-consuming effort to overcome every last weakness and imperfection. They can throw themselves into every conceivable therapy and self-help group. Some can become overly involved in ADD support or advocacy organizations. Parents of ADD children can

---

get hopelessly caught up in making sure that their youngster succeeds academically. Childhoods can be lost in the quest to squeeze out one more ounce of reading or mathematical competence.

What we're trying to warn against is a loss of perspective. When self-improvement gurus sermonize or when self-help books wax poetic about how you can change your life, it all seems so easy and sensible. Follow a few simple steps and your life will improve.

But you shouldn't run your life according to the edicts of a self-help paperback or a motivational seminar. Goals should flow from a sense of what's important to you and what's attainable. While academic and vocational success may be high on the list, ultimately you may find that they shouldn't be as high as you thought. At least not so high that they surpass other priorities less oriented to achievement and efficiency.

OK. We admit it. We want to write the book, *The Seven Habits of People Who Might Not Be All That Effective but Who Can Relax, Be Satisfied with Themselves and Their Loved Ones, and Avoid Spending All Their Time Trying to Be Effective.* We're convinced it will be a publishing event of untold proportions.

No, we're not telling you how your priorities should be arranged. Nor are we going to lecture you on family values, the importance of being happy, or the limitations of material acquisition. We simply hope that the decisions you make strike some balance between pain and pleasure, work and recreation, achievement and love. Because the ultimate goal for most of us shouldn't be to reach a state of perfection. It perhaps should have more to do with achieving closeness, calm, enjoyment, and warmth.

We'll end with another true story:

Terry was a bright, ambitious, and wholly unsuccessful businessman. Although known in his trade for having wonderful ideas, he showed absolutely no capacity to follow through on them competently. His life was a series of failed adventures.

By his mid-30s, Terry became so frustrated with himself that he sought therapy for depression and anxiety. During the course of the initial interviews, the psychologist became suspicious that Terry had ADD. Results of a complete evaluation confirmed that intuition unequivocally.

Terry's professional life took a sharp turn for the better. He started a course of medication and aggressively pursued every avenue he could think of to become more organized. He bought computers, organizers, and dozens of books on maximizing one's potential. He traveled around the country to attend seminars offered by the top preachers of personal effectiveness. He also became intensely (and admirably) involved in forming an Adult ADD support group in his region. In short, he went from being a financial bumbler to an acclaimed whiz on business, motivation, and ADD. For the first time in his career, he also made a considerable amount of money.

But it all came crashing down one day, not more than three years after that initial ADD diagnosis.

Because his wife required brief hospitalization, Terry stayed home to care for their two young children. On the second day, his daughter asked if they could go to the neighborhood park and play on the swings. So off they went.

Terry, of course, brought along his electronic organizer and Dictaphone in case he needed to jot down some notes. And he sat on the bench and watched the children while they played. Well, he watched them only in a technical sense. By his own admission, he was actually deep in thought about how best to conduct that evening's business meeting. He began to list a few of his ideas on his trusty organizer.

Distracted by his children's loud giggles, he looked up to see both of them hanging upside down from the monkey bars. Their little-kid stomachs were sticking out, not to mention snatches of Batman underwear.

He was stunned by how adorable they were and by how little he knew them. He wasn't all that sure what his son was doing in kindergarten or what books he liked to read. He couldn't come up with the name of even one of his daughter's friends or teachers. In trying to overcome his limitations, achieve success, and help others, Terry had lost touch with his family and, once he thought about it, with most other sources of joy.

This epiphany on the playground bench rocked Terry immensely. While he felt that he had lost a sense of balance in his life, he also knew how much he enjoyed the acclaim and his hard-won financial success. Searching for a middle ground took him to the extremes of confusion.

Terry spent the next few weeks talking with his wife, minister, and friends. Over time, he inched his way more toward the center. He resigned from the board of the support group and stopped attending every seminar presented on personal effectiveness. He also lightened his business responsibilities by hiring a manager for one of his enterprises.

But he didn't throw away his organizer. He just doesn't take it to bed with him. And he didn't stop running his business. He simply didn't allow his business to run him.

Last we heard, he was logging a lot more time on that playground bench.

Principle 14

Resources

You will find an especially complete inventory of resources in *Answers to Distraction* and in *A Comprehensive Guide to Attention Deficit Disorder in Adults: Research, Diagnosis, and Treatment* (listed below). The national support groups, CH.A.D.D. and ADDA, are also superb clearinghouses for information.

Most of the materials that follow are available from:

A.D.D. WareHouse
300 NW 70th Avenue
Suite 102
Plantation, FL 33317
800-233-9273

Books and Videos for Adults with ADD—General

Barkley, R. (1994) *ADHD in Adults.* [videotape]. New York: Guilford Press Video.

Hallowell, E. M., and Ratey, J. J. (1994). *Driven to Distraction.* New York, NY: Pantheon Books.

Hallowell, E. M., and Ratey, J. J. (1994). *Answers to Distraction.* New York, NY: Pantheon Books.

Kelly, K., and Ramundo, P. (1995). *You Mean I'm Not Lazy, Stupid, or Crazy?!* New York: Scribners.

Murphy, K. (1995). *Out of the Fog: Treatment Options and Coping Strategies for Adult Attention Deficit Disorder.* New York: Hyperion.

Phelan, T. *Adults with Attention Deficit.* [videotape]. Glen Ellyn, IL: Child Management, Inc. Call 800-442-4453.

Weiss, L. (1992). *Attention Deficit Disorder in Adults: Practical Help for Sufferers and Their Spouses.* Dallas: Taylor Publishing.

Books for Adults with ADD—Higher Education

Nadeau, K. G. (1994). *College Survival Guide for Students with ADD or LD.* New York: Brunner Mazel.

Quinn, P. O. (1994). *ADD and the College Student: A Guide for High School and College Students with Attention Deficit Disorder.* New York: Imagination Press.

Books for Adults with ADD—Legal Issues

Latham, P. S., and Latham, J. D. (1992). *Attention Deficit Disorder and the Law: A Guide for Advocates.* Washington, D.C.: JKL Communications. Call 202-223-5097.

Latham, P. S., and Latham, J. D. eds. (1994). *Succeeding in the Workplace: Attention Deficit Disorder and Learning Disabilities in the Workplace: A Guide for Success.* Washington, D.C.: JKL Communications. Call 202-223-5097.

Latham, P. S., and Latham, J. D. (1994). *Higher Education Services for Students with Learning Disabilities and Attention Deficit Disorder: A Legal Guide.* Washington, D.C.: JKL Communications. Call 202-223-5097.

Legal Resources

Department of Justice
Office of Americans with Disabilities Act
Civil Rights Division
PO Box 66118
Washington, D.C. 20035
202-514-0301

Equal Opportunity Employment Commission
1 Congress Street, 10th Floor, Rm 1001
Boston, MA 02114
800-669-4000

Job Accommodation Network
Box 6080
Morgantown, WV 26506-6080
800-526-7234
800-526-2262 (for Canada)
They consult on legal and practical issues related to accomodations in the workplace.

National Center for Law and Learning Disabilities
PO Box 368
Cabin John, MD 20818
301-469-8308

Office of Civil Rights
330 C Street SW
Room 5000
Washington, D.C. 20202
202-205-5413
Call this office for information about the Americans with Disabilities Act.

Office of Special Education and Rehabilitative Services
330 C Street SW
Switzer Building, Room 3006
Washington, D.C. 20202-2500
202-205-5507
Call this number for help with Section 504 of the Rehabilitation Act or with the Individuals with Disabilities Education Act (IDEA).

Books about Adults with ADD— More Professionally Oriented

While you might not be as interested in these texts, we've listed them in case you need to help a clinician learn more about the disorder:

Barkley, R. A. (1990). *Attention Deficit Hyperactivity Disorder: A Handbook for Diagnosis and Treatment.* New York: Guilford Press.

Gordon, M. (1995). *How to Operate an ADHD Clinic or Subspecialty Practice.* Dewitt, NY: GSI Publications. Call 315-446-4849.

Nadeau, K., ed. (1995). *A Comprehensive Guide to Attention Deficit Disorder in Adults: Research, Diagnosis, and Treatment.* New York: Brunner/Mazel Publishers.

Weiss, G., and Hechtman, L. T. (1986). *Hyperactive Children Grown Up: Empirical Findings and Theoretical Considerations.* New York: Guilford Press.

Wender, P. (1995). *Attention-Deficit Hyperactivity Disorder in Adults.* New York: Oxford University Press.

Organizations for Adults with ADD

ADDult Support Network (ADDA)
PO Box 972
Mentor, OH 44061
800-487-2282

Adult ADD Association
Contact person: Lisa F. Poast
1225 East Sunset Drive, Suite 640
Bellingham, WA 98226-3529
360-647-6681
Acts as a general referral source.

Adult Attention Deficit Foundation
Box 217
Ortonville, MI 48462
810-540-6335

CH.A.D.D. (Children and Adults with Attention Deficit Disorder)
National Headquarters
Suite 308
499 NW 70th Avenue
Plantation, FL 33317
305-487-3700
CH.A.D.D. is the largest support organization for all individuals who live with or work with ADD.

Learning Disabilities Association of America (LDA)
4156 Library Road
Pittsburgh, PA 15234
412-341-1515

Adult ADD Newsletter

ADD-ONS Newsletter
Mary Daum, Editor
PO Box 675
Frankfort, IL 60423
815-469-8567
(Subscriptions available for $20.)

ADDult News
Mary Jane Johnson, Editor
2620 Ivy Place
Toledo, OH 46313
E-mail address: 75200.1463@compuserve.com

Attention!
Available to members of CH.A.D.D.
Call 305-587-3700.

ADD On-Line

In our quest to find resources, we stumbled upon a gold mine of ADD support in cyberspace. Believe it or not, there's a remarkable array of chat rooms, conferences, and networkings available to you. At the time we're writing this book, America Online (AOL) seems to have the most extensive selection.

America Online: You'll currently find 16 regularly scheduled events for those involved with ADD. They include chats for men, women, partners, children, teens, parents, and educators. You can find the latest schedule if you use the Keyword function: Type IMH, then check the Daily Living section. You can also use E-mail to contact the following hosts: SusanS29, Debette, Annie12345, MaryDee, JimAMS, or EricNJB.

Prodigy: This service has an ADD bulletin board in the Medical Support area. Type Jump: Medical Support and look for the Attention Deficit Topic. There is also an Attention Deficit chat room, where members can chat live about ADD 24 hours a day. Type Jump: Chat.

CompuServe: Go to GO ADD or E-mail 70006.101@compuserve.com.

World Wide Web: Type http://www.interconnect.com/oneaddplace/

Organizations That Help with Organization

The National Association of Professional Organizers
1033 LaPosada Drive, Suite 220
Austin, TX 78752-3880
512-206-0151
They provide lists of professional organizers in your area.

The National Coaching Network
PO Box 353
Lafayette Hill, PA 19444
NCN provides coaching for ADD adults, trains individuals to become coaches, and offers ADD-oriented educational services.

Books/Videos for Parents of ADD Children

Because ADD adults often have ADD children, we've included materials about youngsters:

Barkley, R. A. (1992). *ADHD—What Do We Know?* [videotape]. New York: Guilford Press.

Barkley, R. A. (1992). *ADHD—What Can We Do?* [videotape]. New York: Guilford Press.

Barkley, R. A. (1995). *Taking Charge of ADHD: The Complete Authoritative Guide for Parents.* New York: Guilford Press.

Forehand, R. L., and McMahon, R. J. (1981). *Helping the Noncompliant Child.* New York: Guilford Press.

Fowler, M. C. (1990). *Maybe You Know My Child.* New York: Birch Lane Press.

Gordon, M. (1990). *ADHD/Hyperactivity: A Consumer's Guide.* DeWitt, NY: GSI Publications.

Ingersoll, B. (1988). *Your Hyperactive Child.* New York: Doubleday.

Ingersoll, B. D., and Goldstein, S. (1993). *Attention Deficit Disorder and Learning Disabilities: Realities, Myths, and Controversial Treatments.* New York, New York: Doubleday.

Parker, H. C. (1988). *The ADD Hyperactivity Workbook for Parents, Teachers, and Kids.* Plantation, FL: Impact Publications.

Phelan, T. (1990). *1–2–3 Magic: Training Your Preschoolers and Preteens to Do What You Want!* Glen Ellyn, IL: Child Management, Inc. Call 800-442-4453.

Wodrich, D. L. (1994). *Attention Deficit Hyperactivity Disorder: What Every Parent Wants to Know.* Baltimore: Paul H. Brooks Publishing Co. PO Box 10624, Baltimore, MD 21285-0624

Books/Videos for Children

The following materials can be ordered from GSI Publications by calling 315-446-4849 or by using the order form at the end of this book:

Gordon, M. (1991). *Jumpin' Johnny Get Back to Work!: A Child's Guide to ADHD/Hyperactivity.* DeWitt, NY: GSI Publications.

Gordon, M. (1992). *My Brother's a World-Class Pain: A Sibling's Guide to ADHD/Hyperactivity.* DeWitt, NY: GSI Publications.

Gordon, M. (1992). *I Would If I Could: A Teenager's Guide to ADHD/Hyperactivity.* DeWitt, NY: GSI Publications.

Gordon, M. (1994). *Jumpin' Johnny Get Back to Work!: A Child's Guide to ADHD/Hyperactivity* [videotape]. DeWitt, NY: GSI Publications.

Books in Spanish for Parents and Children

Gordon, M. (1995). *Juancito Salterín ¡A tu Trabajo de Nuevo! Un Guia para Niños con Desorden de Hiperactividad y Déficit de Atención (DHDA).* DeWitt, NY: GSI Publications. Call 315-446-4849 or use the order form at the end of this book.

Parker, H. C. (1994). *Cuaderno de Trabajo para Padres, Maestros y Niños Sobre el Trastorno de Bajo Nivel de Atención (ADD) o Hiperactividad.* Plantation, FL: Specialty Press.

Parent and Teacher Support Organizations

CH.A.D.D. (Children and Adults with Attention Deficit Disorder)
National Headquarters
Suite 308
499 NW 70th Avenue
Plantation, FL 33317
305-487-3700

Learning Disabilities Association of America (LDA)
4156 Library Road
Pittsburgh, PA 15234
412-341-1515

To order one of our books or for more information, just complete the order form, tear it off, and mail it back to us.

Name: _____

Street: _____

City: _____State: _____Zip: _____

❑ **The Down & Dirty Guide to Adult ADD**...........**$16.95** ea.
A No Nonsense Book for Adults

❑ **ADHD / Hyperactivity:** ....**$14.95** ea.
A Consumer's Guide For Parents and Teachers

❑ **Jumpin' Johnny Get Back to Work!** ....**$10.00** ea.
A Child's Guide to ADHD/Hyperactivity

❑ **Jumpin' Johnny Video & Book Set** ....**$45.00** ea.
Set including VHS Video & Book

❑ **Juanito Saltarín ¡A Tu Trabajo De Nuevo!** ......**$11.00** ea.
Spanish version of 'Jumpin Johnny'

❑ **I Would If I Could:** ....**$12.50** ea.
A Teenager's Guide To ADHD/Hyperactivity

❑ **My Brother's a World Class Pain** ....**$11.00** ea.
A Sibling's Guide to ADHD/Hyperactivity

❑ **I'd Rather Be with a Real Mom Who Loves Me**..**$12.00**
A Story for Foster Children

❑ **Teaching the Child with ADD** .... **$150.00** ea.
A Slide Program for In-Service Teacher Training

❑ **How to Operate an ADHD Clinic
or Subspecialty Practice** ....**$59.95** ea.
For Professionals

❑ **Publications Brochure**..**Free!**
Complete descriptions of all our books & ordering information.

Sub Total: _____
Add 10% to your order for shipping: _____
Add 20% for shipping to Canada: _____
(N.Y.S. residents add 7% tax): _____
Total: _____

> For shipping outside the Continental U.S. or Canada, please call us at (315) 446-4849 and ask for the shipping charges.

❑ Check enclosed, payable to GSI Publications
❑ Mastercard ❑ Visa   Expiration Date: _____
Card Number:_____

Cardholder's Signature

GSI Publications, Inc.
P.O. Box 746, DeWitt, New York 13214-0746
Phone: (315) 446-4849 Fax: (315) 446-2012
Call us for quantity discounts on large orders.

GSI
PUBLICATIONS, INC.

PUBLICATIONS, INC.

BUSINESS REPLY MAIL

FIRST-CLASS MAIL PERMIT NO. 5689 SYRACUSE, NY

POSTAGE WILL BE PAID BY ADDRESSEE

GSI Publications

P.O. Box 746

DeWitt, New York 13214-9938

To order one of our books or for more information, just complete the order form, tear it off, and mail it back to us.

Name: _____

Street: _____

City: _____State: _____Zip: _____

☐ **The Down & Dirty Guide to Adult ADD**...........**$16.95** ea.
A No Nonsense Book for Adults

☐ **ADHD / Hyperactivity:** ....**$14.95** ea.
A Consumer's Guide For Parents and Teachers

☐ **Jumpin' Johnny Get Back to Work!** ....**$10.00** ea.
A Child's Guide to ADHD/Hyperactivity

☐ **Jumpin' Johnny Video & Book Set** ....**$45.00** ea.
Set including VHS Video & Book

☐ **Juanito Saltarín ¡A Tu Trabajo De Nuevo!** ....**$11.00** ea.
Spanish version of 'Jumpin Johnny'

☐ **I Would If I Could:** ....**$12.50** ea.
A Teenager's Guide To ADHD/Hyperactivity

☐ **My Brother's a World Class Pain** ....**$11.00** ea.
A Sibling's Guide to ADHD/Hyperactivity

☐ **I'd Rather Be with a Real Mom Who Loves Me**..**$12.00**
A Story for Foster Children

☐ **Teaching the Child with ADD** .... **$150.00** ea.
A Slide Program for In-Service Teacher Training

☐ **How to Operate an ADHD Clinic**
or Subspecialty Practice ....**$59.95** ea.
For Professionals

☐ **Publications Brochure**...**Free!**
Complete descriptions of all our books & ordering information.

Sub Total: _____

Add 10% to your order for shipping: _____

Add 20% for shipping to Canada: _____

(N.Y.S. residents add 7% tax): _____

Total: _____

For shipping outside the Continental U.S. or Canada, please call us at (315) 446-4849 and ask for the shipping charges.

☐ Check enclosed, payable to GSI Publications
☐ Mastercard ☐ Visa   Expiration Date: _____
Card Number:_____

Cardholder's Signature

GSI Publications, Inc.
P.O. Box 746, DeWitt, New York 13214-0746
Phone: (315) 446-4849 Fax: (315) 446-2012
Call us for quantity discounts on large orders.

GSI
PUBLICATIONS, INC.

PUBLICATIONS, INC.

BUSINESS REPLY MAIL

FIRST-CLASS MAIL PERMIT NO. 5689 SYRACUSE, NY

POSTAGE WILL BE PAID BY ADDRESSEE

GSI Publications

P.O. Box 746

DeWitt, New York 13214-9938